THE JESUS
CONTACT

THE JESUS CONTACT

One womans spiritual journey from
Metaphysical to Christ through
actual encounters with Jesus

LINDA K. MILLER

Columbus, Ohio

The Jesus Contact: One womans spiritual journey from Metaphysical to Christ through actual encounters with Jesus

Published by Gatekeeper Press

2167 Stringtown Rd, Suite 109

Columbus, OH 43123-2989

www.GatekeeperPress.com

Cover Designer: Ronchon Villaester

Editor: Madison Drake

Formatter: Joshua Kaplan

Special Thanks to: Nicole Dudley

ISBN (paperback): 9781642379433

eISBN: 9781642379440

DISCLAIMER

Some names and identifying details have been changed to protect the privacy of individuals. Accounts are based on author's memory of said events and some dialog may have been recreated. Author and publisher do not assume and hereby disclaim any liability to any party for any loss, damage, or disruption caused by errors, omissions, or any information in this book. Author will not compensate you in anyway whatsoever if you happen to suffer a loss, inconvenience, or damage because of any information in this book. Thank you.

DEDICATION

To the One who knows me inside and out
and loves me anyway.

ACKNOWEDGEMENTS

I would like to thank the Father,
Son, and Holy Spirit for
carrying me through this journey,
my husband for all of your love, never ending
patience, and support. I would also like to thank
Darleen, Olivia, Marlene, and Angelo for
your positive advice and encouragement.
I would also like to thank the staff at Gatekeeper
Press for all of your professional guidance and quality
production in the making of this special book.

Contents

THE SECRET'S OUT

CHAPTER ONE

I HAD FRIED CHICKEN and all the fixings ready and on the table. This was going to be one dinner I would never forget. Not because of my fabulous home cooking—it was takeout—but because of what was going to transpire in a few short moments. My husband and I invited the pastor and his wife to our home this evening. But this was not a social call; it was all business for me. I needed the Pastor's advice on an issue I had been struggling with for a long time. I was living with a secret. I had kept this secret hidden for years, mostly out of fear of what other people would think of me. Fear is a horrible companion and I was ready to cut ties with it. What I had experienced could fill a book, and I was contemplating writing one. It was time to bring my story to light, even though my life would never be the same once I told it.

The Pastor and his wife arrived right on time and we exchanged polite chitchat while we made our way into the kitchen. As we took our seats around the table, my hands were shaking. I had played this scene over in my mind a thousand times, and now it was actually happening. How was this gracious couple going to react? I had no idea. They were a conservative, middle-aged pair who had dedicated their lives to serving the Lord. I had known them for years and this evening just might change how our relationship continued. I was taking a risk divulging my story with this Baptist preacher, he could easily oust me from his church for what I was about to tell him. It was one of the fears that kept me quiet for so long. I loved my church family and I really didn't want to be asked to leave, but what I had to share was worth the risk.

Pastor said grace. Lord help me. Was I ready for this? Now was not the time to second guess myself, but once I opened my mouth, there would be no turning back. I wanted to crawl under the table and hide, but knew my story needed to be told. I knew it could help and would hopefully enlighten others, even though I could be judged for telling it. Some people might even think I was crazy, and, at that moment, I wasn't so sure myself.

As the food was passed around the table, I took a deep breath and glanced over at my husband, Bob. He gave me a reassuring smile, then his "it's now or never" look. Okay. Here we go. I waited for a lull in the conversation, and then cleared my throat. "Pastor, the reason we asked you over tonight is because I'm thinking of writing a book and I need your opinion on whether I should do it or not." Did I really hear myself just say that? I just started the conversation that was about to change my life. Lord have mercy on me. I nervously continued, "What I'm about to tell you I've only told a few people. It's something I've kept quiet for over fifteen years and I think it's time I shared it."

That got their attention. I glanced around to see all eyes were on me. I took another deep breath.

"I guess I should start at the beginning. When I was seventeen years old…" and I was off and running. I was so anxious; I could hardly look at them. It was hard to get the words out. Thank goodness for Pastor's wife, she was supportive and encouraged me to continue. And I did. For over forty-five minutes, I poured my heart out as they quietly listened and ate their dinner. Mine grew cold.

Through tears, confessions and even laughter, I disclosed everything. I didn't leave any details out. My mind was reeling and I was emotionally exhausted. I felt like I had just stepped off a rollercoaster, a little woozy, but glad I took the ride. Now, my testimony was finished—maybe I was too. At that point, it didn't matter because I had finally let the bird out of the cage. This was the first time I told someone outside my inner circle my entire story and it was liberating.

But the nagging reality was that I now had to deal with the consequences of revealing my secret. I was hoping for the best, but also expecting the worst. I just took the biggest risk of my life and I didn't know if I crashed and burned or not. What was Pastor thinking? This was a man I had respected for over ten years. I knew I could trust his decision to be honest and biblically based, but I also knew he wouldn't pull any punches. Did he think I was unstable or did he find my story valid? Was my experience worth sharing or was he going to throw me out of his church? I sincerely felt voicing my story was something God wanted me to do and I truly needed the Pastor's theological opinion. The crucial moment of this meeting was finally here, and the anticipation was killing me.

I hesitantly looked over at the Pastor; he was hard to read. I had just given this faithful man of God a lot to process and he was mulling it over. I couldn't wait any longer. I needed to know what he thought about this whole thing and I needed to know *now*. My stomach was churning as I found the courage to ask him the most important question of the evening. Looking him directly in the eye, I bit the bullet and with sweaty palms asked, "Well, what do you think?"

He paused for a moment, and then shifted in his chair. It felt like an eternity. I thought I was going to pass out from the suspense. Please, please, *please* tell me something good. I watched and waited, a mere few seconds that seemed to take forever. Gradually, a smile came over his face.

"Write the book," he said. "I don't think you have a choice."

Every story has a beginning, some start with an event or an experience. Mine started with a dream. Funny thing about dreams, they can take you on an unexpected journey and change your world in ways you never imagined. I was seventeen and it was 1978.

I was living with my parents on a farm about forty miles north of Detroit. As a typical teenager, I was busy with school and friends. I went to high school in a small, country town where everybody knew everybody. The whole town would turn out for Friday night football games and we had an ice cream stand where everyone seemed to congregate during the summer. There also was a mom and pop diner on Main Street where I ate more than my fair share of chili cheese fries. The fall season in our community included Harvest Week where students could take time off from studies to help in the fields. Many of the kids, like me, had farm chores at home before their day started at school.

My family raised Arabian horses and even though it was a lot of work, it was fun having a barn full of horses at home. Spring time was foaling season, my favorite time of the year. Staying up 'til all hours of the night waiting for the mares to give birth and helping with the process was an amazing experience. That first nicker between a mare and her foal is a priceless event to witness; I never got tired of it. As the herd grew, we had about ten mares in our barn. We also had a stallion which we owned with another investor. We stabled him at the partner's ranch which was fine with me—stallions are a handful.

I was also involved with showing German Shepherds. I

enjoyed training dogs to show, especially the puppies. My folks agreed to build a kennel for me if I would take care of the day to day expenses of raising them. To keep it manageable, I only had a few dogs, and worked Saturdays at my parent's photography studio to pay for dog food, vet bills, and show expenses. I didn't mind the financial obligation; I loved my dogs.

Having horses and dogs was a wonderful learning opportunity. These were living creatures that were totally dependent on you for all their needs. I acquired the hands-on skills necessary for their care, such as grooming, giving vaccinations, treating injuries, and even assisting the veterinarians with medical procedures. I also experienced all sorts of emotional highs and lows, from the joy of births to the heartbreak of deaths and everything in between. It taught me responsibility and that time with our animals is short.

Needless to say, my days were pretty full with school, friends, homework, barn chores and dog training. Looking back, I wonder how I fit it all in. When evening rolled around, I had no trouble sleeping at night—until the dreams started. I wasn't tormented with nightmares or night terrors, my affliction was different. My dreams came true. Literally.

I remember the first time it happened. I had had a dream about a woman whom we bought a horse from. Occasionally she would stop by to visit the horse, as she had raised him from a foal and was still emotionally attached. My parents understood their special bond and allowed her visits; they just asked her to call before she came. In my dream, she arrived unannounced, all smiles as she got out of her car wearing a purple sweater with blue jeans and tennis shoes. She waved hello to me and I returned the gesture. That's all there was to the dream, just a short glimpse of the scene.

When I awoke the next morning, I recalled the dream

but didn't think anything of it. You can imagine my surprise when, later that day, I watched her unexpectedly drive up to the stable and get out of her car wearing the exact outfit as in my dream! How was that possible?! It was crazy! And a little spooky.

The premonition dreams occurred regularly. I would have one every other week or so. They usually were just fleeting glances of a scene or a conversation, but they always played out the following day, precisely as I had dreamed them. Déjà vu moments with a twist. It was surreal. I wasn't able to change the outcome of the dreams; it was like being a puppet on a string with someone else calling the shots. I was reliving dreams everywhere I went: school, home, a friend's house, restaurants; no place was safe from the experiences.

I didn't understand how this phenomenon was happening to me. I talked to my parents about it, they didn't understand either. I think they were hoping it was a phase I would outgrow. They definitely thought it was "unusual". No kidding. Try living with it! When I went to bed at night, I never knew if I was going to have "one of those" dreams. If I did dream of familiar people or places, I would spend the next day wondering if I was going to relive it. It was not an enjoyable super power.

The dreams continued for months and were starting to give me anxiety. I didn't talk about them with my friends at school, I knew how kids could be and I didn't want to be made fun of or labeled as a freak. I was smart enough to know this was something I was better off keeping to myself. The dreams were completely out of my control and I didn't know what to do. I needed help, but where would I begin to look for it - a doctor? I didn't think "How to Cure ESP Dreams" was a course they taught at medical school. I had nowhere to turn. I was tired of being a player in a game I didn't ask to participate in; I just wanted the dreams to stop. Then one day, they miraculously did.

I had called a friend that had recently moved to another state. She was one of the few people I could trust with my "special gift". During our conversation, I shared with her the dream I had the night before. This dream was different. It didn't contain any familiar faces, but the dream haunted me all day and I couldn't shake it. I just needed to vent.

The dream began on a country road lined with big oak trees on a bright, sunny day. The road continued over an old stone bridge with a classic babbling brook running underneath. It was a very charming scene except for the horrific disaster unfolding right in the middle of it. A school bus, filled with children, had flipped over on its side. Grade school kids were strewn about on the grassy ditches, some badly injured. It was total chaos. Kids screaming, first responders arriving—a real nightmare. The dream frightened me so bad I woke up from it. I heard my friend gasp on the other end of the phone.

"I saw your dream!" she said. "I was driving home today and I saw that accident! It was horrible! There were people everywhere. Traffic was all backed up and the police finally routed us around it. It was a mess."

I couldn't believe what I was hearing. After I hung up the phone, I collapsed in a chair and sobbed. Why did I dream of that accident? I couldn't prevent it. What was the purpose of having to witness it? If these bizarre dreams were becoming tragic predictions I couldn't do anything about, I definitely wanted out.

I was frustrated, angry and scared. I was on a runaway train and didn't know how to get off.

Through my tears, I desperately cried out to God, "If this is a gift, I don't want it! I didn't ask for it and I don't understand it! I can't take it anymore! Please make this stop!"

When my tears finally subsided, I felt a calmness wash over me. After being so upset, I didn't understand how I could feel such peace. I believe God answered my prayer that day because I never had "one of those" dreams again.

It was a wonderful relief. Life was slowly returning back to normal. As each day went by, I realized I could put the dreams behind me. It took a few months, but the anxiety left and I felt like I could breathe again. By this time, I had graduated high school and was now working full time with my parents at the photography studio while showing my dogs on the weekends.

Traveling with show dogs was an education in itself. I learned to be independent and how to handle myself in a competitive atmosphere. Anytime you have a group of people bound together by competition, you see the good and the bad in humanity. The dog show world was no exception; there was cheating and animal abuse, but also dedication to better the breed by good, upright people. I saw both sides and it gave me an insight to human nature and what some competitors were capable of. I didn't believe in cheating to win, if I couldn't come by it honestly, I didn't need it. I would never have compromised my animals with drugs or abusive training techniques for a blue ribbon and I had a hard time understanding how others could. I learned many lessons early by being involved with dog showing which helped me later on in life.

So, now my schedule was pretty full of working forty hours a week and spending more time on the road with my dogs. But I no longer had to contend with the dreams. I was finally free of them. Unfortunately, my reprieve didn't last long because, before I knew it, I had another nocturnal invader to deal with. And I didn't see this one coming either.

It was an uneventful day of work and my usual routine of dog training and chores. That evening, I went to bed around the same time as I usually did. At two o' clock in the morning, I woke up from a sound sleep for no apparent reason. When I opened my eyes, I caught a glimpse of something at the foot of my bed. I turned to get a better look at what caught my attention, and found an old man dressed in a worn-out flannel shirt and overalls staring back at me. I didn't recognize the man and he appeared transparent and chalky white. You got it—a real, live ghost. He didn't move or speak; he just stood there and watched me with a sad, despondent look on his face.

You would think my first reaction would be to scream bloody murder and run for my life, but I didn't. Odd as it was, I felt sorry for him. I sensed he meant no harm and didn't feel threatened in any way. His presence unexpectedly had a calming effect, so I just nonchalantly rolled over and went back to sleep.

However, I can tell you the conversation at the breakfast table the next morning was a little lively. I wasn't rattled during the experience, but when I had time to reflect on what had actually happened, I had a change of heart. Seeing an apparition wasn't something I wanted as a regular occurrence—once was enough for me. But how do you stop a ghost from reappearing if it decides it wants to? It was something I didn't have control over and if there was such a thing as ghost repellant spray, I would have bought a case of it. For weeks, I slept with a nightlight on.

So here I am, a young woman having paranormal experiences I can't explain, first the dreams, then the ghost. To say I was curious about the supernatural would be an understatement.   I just wanted to understand what in the world was going on and why it happened to me. Who wouldn't? I didn't know of anyone else who had experienced dreams like mine, I knew it wasn't normal. And as for the ghost, I think everyone knows someone who's got a ghost story; but when it happens to you, it's a different story altogether. Even though the sighting only lasted a few, brief moments, it had a huge impact on me. So, with an inquisitive mind and a library card, I set out on a journey of spiritual enlightenment. I was on a mission to find the truth. I just had no idea what a wild ride it would be.

THE SEARCH FOR
TRUTH BEGINS

CHAPTER TWO

W HEN I WAS a teenager, the internet didn't exist. If
you wanted to research something, you headed to
the local library or bookstore. It was natural for me
to start my journey with books, having been teased on more
than one occasion for always having one in my back pocket.
Books were uncharted adventures in my eyes; you could open
a book and be transported to a new world within minutes,
fiction or non-fiction, it didn't matter. I loved books and spent
a lot of time with my nose in one.

My search for answers began with the Bible as I was raised
as a Christian, even though my family currently didn't go to
church. Both of my parents had a Christian upbringing and
realized the importance of instilling that in me, which I'm glad
they did. Dad always said grace at the dinner table and would
finish the prayer with "… and bless this food and the hands
that prepared it. Amen." I loved that prayer because if I helped
my mom in the kitchen that day, I got an extra blessing.

As a little girl, we lived next door to an Evangelical church
and my folks always made sure I went to church on Sundays,
even though sometimes they didn't go with me. They were
operating their photography studio out of the home at the
time and Sundays meant long hours catching up on business.

Our house had a camera room and sales room located at one end with the photo labs in the basement and I remember many weekends my Mom and Dad would be downstairs working on orders. So, I would often go to church without them. Sunday school was a fun place where we played games and did crafts, and I learned about Jesus. But when I was in the fifth grade, we moved and without a church conveniently within walking distance, my Bible lessons were put on hold.

The lessons picked up again when I was in my early teen years. My parents let me spend a few summer vacations with my aunt, uncle and cousin on their farm in northern Michigan. My Aunt Marsha was a devout Baptist who never missed a Sunday morning or Wednesday evening service. We always had a good time at her church, and I saw firsthand how much she loved the Lord. Her unwavering devotion made a lasting impression on me.

I loved to hear my aunt tell stories about her life. One of my favorites took place when she was in the process of opening a restaurant. She and my uncle purchased an old, run down diner and poured all their money into revamping it and getting it ready to open for business. On the day of the final inspection, the inspector handed her a report filled with bad news. The grill in the kitchen would have to be replaced. My aunt was devastated; they didn't have the money to buy a new commercial grill. She was so close to her dream and right before the grand opening, it was dashed away. When the inspector left, she sat down at one of the tables and bawled her heart out. What was she going to do? She was tapped out. She started to pray. She knew the Lord was in control and was the only one at this point who could help her.

Just as she finished her prayer, the front door of the restaurant opened. It was the handyman she had hired to help with the renovations. He saw her crying.

"Marsha, what's wrong?" he asked.

"We're shut down. The inspector said we need a new grill and I don't have the money. We're done."

"Marsha," he proceeded to say. "I was just down at the nursing home and they're replacing the grill in their kitchen today, and they don't know what to do with the old one. It's still good and I bet we can get it for next to nothing. They might even give it to us if we haul it away." Her prayers were answered! They were able to acquire the grill that same day and get it running in time for the grand opening.

"Anything is possible with God," she would always say, and she knew it from personal experience.

I never shared my dreams or the ghost sighting with my Aunt Marsha. I was afraid she would think the devil was somehow involved and I didn't want to hear a lecture on it. These experiences weren't anything I was conjuring up with the help of Satan; they were things that just happened to me, and besides none of my experiences felt evil, they were just unexplained.

Back to my search for answers—I knew the Bible contained passages that included dreams. I flipped through the Old Testament and read about dreams where an angel or God spoke to someone, or prophetic dreams that needed to be interpreted, but unfortunately, didn't find any information on dreams that came true the next day like mine had. After consulting the Bible without much resolve, I continued my mission of truth with more books—paranormal books. I found a variety of books on premonitions and ghost sightings. One book led to another and the more I read, the more I wanted to read. This was fascinating stuff.

I was spending more time in the occult section of the bookstore looking for material on the unexplained. My journey was taking me down a new path and I wasn't even aware of where I was being led. There was an enticing, celestial world out there and I wanted a glimpse into this place, after all it was where we were going to spend eternity. I simply wanted to know what happened to us once we died. Where did we go? What did we do over there? Were our loved ones there to meet us? I was soon reading books on angels, spirit guides, near death experiences and psychics. The other side and all its secrets held me captive.

Before long, merely reading about the spirit world wasn't enough. I wanted to get my feet wet and experience the intriguing things I was reading about. It was exciting to think I could have personal messages given to me from the other side. I was ready to take my education farther; one more step on my path of enlightenment. I never thought about where I was headed on this journey, I was just enjoying the ride.

A friend took me to see my first psychic when I was nineteen years old. She knew a woman who was highly recommended and was supposed to be a very accurate medium. I was eager to have a professional reading, a magical glimpse into the future for a mere forty bucks. What was in the cards for me? I was soon to find out.

When we arrived at the psychic's house, an elderly man wearing a plaid shirt and red suspenders let us in. He told us his wife would be with us in a minute and we could wait with him in the living room. The two of us took a seat on the sofa while he plopped down in a recliner. He wasn't one for conversation and the silence was growing a little uncomfortable.

Then out of the blue, he announces, "I've got a dog that bites and he's lying behind that couch you're sitting on." *What?* Was this guy for real? I looked at my friend, she was just as surprised as I was. Our host continued as he fumbled with something in his chair, "But don't worry, if he comes out of there, I'll just use this!" and he yanked out a cattle prod from between the cushions. *Seriously!?* Who keeps a cattle prod in their chair? And what kind of crazy lets a vicious dog hide behind the furniture? When it came time for our individual readings, my friend didn't hesitate to go first. Waiting in that living room for her to get done was the longest half hour of my life.

When it finally was my turn, a sweet, grey-haired lady led me down a hallway to a screened in porch near the back of the house. I wondered how she could possibly be married to the cattle prod wielder in the other room.

She laughed off my question about their mystery dog, saying, "Yes, he bites but not very often, he usually has to be provoked. If you leave him alone, he's fine." Alrighty then, enough about the dog, it was time for my reading.

We sat down in overstuffed chairs as she set a timer and began to tell me things she couldn't have possibly known about me. She "saw" I traveled with my dogs and knew how many I had. She also knew about an uncle of mine who had just died, and she enlightened me about the ghost I saw in my bedroom. She explained the spirit was a farmer who once owned the property we lived on. He committed suicide by hanging himself in the old barn that still stood across the street from our house. On the night of my encounter, he was just visiting his property. I was impressed! By the time my reading was finished, I was convinced psychics were the real deal— well, okay, maybe not *all* of them, but this lady had a gift for sure.

After that first reading, I started going to psychic fairs on my own, just occasionally. I knew I had to be careful; there were plenty of so-called psychics out there that were nothing but cons. They would predict all sorts of bad news and then ask you for more money so they could pray for you and remove all the evil curses supposedly surrounding you. I was aware that many people had handed over a lot of money to these scammers, and I wasn't going to be one of them. I felt sorry for the victims, mostly women, who depended on psychics for guidance. It was a bad habit to get into and it wasn't my intention in visiting them. I was on a mission for spiritual answers.

I gravitated towards the spiritualists, those who could communicate with the other side. I wasn't concerned with learning about my future, I'd let God take care of that; I wanted to hear messages from my spirit guides and family members who had passed over. The readings gave me hope there actually was life after death. It was my proof Heaven existed. To have a psychic recognize your deceased grandma by name and relay warm wishes from her was wonderful. It made me feel well loved knowing my relatives wanted to reach out to me from the spirit world.

Watching the techniques the mediums used to connect with spirits was intriguing as well. Some used an object to focus on, like a crystal ball or tarot cards. Others closed their eyes while they carried on conversations with the spirits, and some just sat and talked normally, only pausing to listen to a voice you couldn't hear. I absorbed it all. It was mesmerizing to witness the process.

I also continued to read about spirituality and, over time, began to blend in the New Age beliefs with my Christian background. These new teachings were positive and easy to apply to my everyday life. I learned we were all on a journey of spiritual growth and there were many paths to enlightenment. We were all born from spirit and would return to spirit when our journey here was completed. We weren't placed on this earth by accident, but we all had a purpose as both a student and a teacher. It is all about love: abiding in love, projecting love, and seeing it in everything. We were all connected and one with the Universe. I innocently embraced these ideas and many others as they just felt right to me. I enjoyed the upbeat teachings without all the Hell, fire and damnation. It was all good—or so I thought.

As I was venturing out spiritually, I also wanted to try living out on my own. I was now in my mid-twenties and thought I was ready for a new chapter in my life. I had recently retired from showing dogs and my folks were getting out of the horse business. I loved the life I had on the farm, but it was time to make a change. Our family had just grown weary of the amount of work involved and the 24/7 responsibility of raising animals. Sometimes you have to let go of things, even if you love them, when they hold you back from moving forward.

I decided to move to the outskirts of Detroit, closer to work. My parents had relocated the business many years ago to a commercial building they had built with an outdoor studio on the premises. Not having to drive an hour to work every day was a blessing. I missed the horses terribly, but I still had my favorite dogs with me and living near a big city was a new adventure full of social and cultural events. I was now attending art openings, live theater, and all sorts of concerts. There was always something to do and somewhere to go. This was certainly a different lifestyle than the country offered, and I embraced every minute of it. Gone were the days of breaking ice buckets in the freezing winter weather, now I only had to worry about breaking my neck in four-inch heels.

It was during this time that I met my husband. A coworker at the studio introduced us. Bob was ruggedly handsome with blonde hair and blue eyes and I liked his sense of humor right away. He had a laugh that was contagious and a glint in his eye that hinted he was one step away from doing something he probably shouldn't. We started dating after he passed the dog test (if your dogs don't approve of who you bring home, walk away—no, run away as fast as you can).

I soon discovered that Bob and I had a lot in common. We came from similar backgrounds as we both went directly into the work force upon graduating high school and we both worked with our families; my profession being photography and his was finish carpentry. It was nice to be around someone who understood the dynamics of working in a family business. Bob was a responsible man's man, who could balance a heavy workload and still take time to enjoy life. I admired that. It didn't take long for us to fall in love and by the time I was thirty, we were married.

As Bob and I were getting settled into our new home, my parents were looking to retire from photography. They had started the business before I was born and after forty-five years, they were ready to hand over the torch. I couldn't run the business by myself, but together with a long-time coworker as a partner, it was a possibility. After much consideration, the two of us purchased the studio. My responsibilities were the sales staff, art department, and inner office, while my partner oversaw the photographers, photo lab and the school contracts we obtained. I was grateful for the opportunity as I never thought I would be fortunate enough to have my own business. It was a huge commitment, but I welcomed the challenge of being a business owner. Life was steadily moving along, and so was my growth in spirituality.

Whenever I attended a psychic reading, I would receive messages from spirit guides through a medium, but I wanted to hear these messages firsthand, for myself. It's not that I didn't trust the psychic's ability, I was just curious to have my own spiritual experiences. If other people could connect with the spirit world, why couldn't I? Not everyone who was a psychic came by it naturally, there had to be methods of learning this "craft". With a little searching on the internet, I found a set of training tapes produced by a well-known psychic. I purchased them and began to teach myself. With an open mind and a little practice, it didn't take long and I was able to perform the types of spiritual meditations I had only read about previously. My journey for spiritual truth was really taking off now!

I meditated about twice a month. It was amazing. I would begin each meditation by sitting crossed-legged on the floor and aligning my chakras, a line of energy fields within the body. Once my energy was balanced, I would say a prayer of protection and envision myself wrapped in a heavenly, white light. Next, I would concentrate on my breathing. The mantra, "in with the good, out with the bad" would be repeated with each inhale and exhale. After a few minutes, my body would be so relaxed I couldn't feel myself in it. At this point, I was able to cross over to the other side and meet with my spirit guides.

I had two spirit guides. The first guide I met was Sister Mary, a kind and gentle spirit who was an older woman, short in stature. She always wore the same modest dress with a light blue head covering and spoke with an accent I didn't recognize. My other guide was Two White Feathers, a well-built Native American who presented himself in a traditional deerskin outfit. He was middle-aged, gruff and grumpy, even though he had a big heart underneath all that bluster.

They would wait for me at our designated spiritual meeting place, which was a destination of my own creation. I chose a scenic location on a grassy hilltop overlooking a tranquil, seascape below. Vintage ships sailed in the distance and horses scattered the hill side, contently grazing (of course there were horses—after all, it was *my* happy place). The messages they shared with me were positive and enlightening. I wrote many of them down and referred to them often. Sister Mary spoke more than Two White Feathers and I took her advice to heart. Here are a few of her words:

"Love comes in all forms. Understand this about love. Love is universal. Animal, human, spirit it does not matter, it is in everything. It is all the same love. Do not be afraid. Learn to see the love in everything. It is there. It is in you as well. Learn to see. Learn to live. Live with love. Open your heart. Open your life. This you can do."

"When an effort is made, new doors are opened up. You are ready for the next step of enlightenment. Always try. You may not always succeed, but you will learn. You will grow. Take a step—a step forward on your path. Let love show you how."

"The time is now. This is how you live your life. Now. In the now. You create and can change the now, but not the past. Leave it there. Enjoy the now, it's all you have. Look forward to the future. Plan other 'nows'. Live your now with love. Send love to each 'now' you're in. Life is made of now moments."

"Ask to see the love and you will see it. Ask to see forgiveness and you will see it. Ask to see the pain and you will see it. You see what you look for. Be careful of your quest."

"This is a day of new beginnings, each day is. Trust in the love. Trust in the life. You have much to offer. Your beginnings are now. Enjoy the now. It is your time. Take time for fun. Much can be done in fun. Don't be afraid to kick up your heels. Laugh much. It fills your heart with good things. Each day is a new beginning. Always remember this. You create a new you each day."

"Life is uncertain. Do not be afraid of the uncertainty. It is your chance to grow and be strong. Life is full of uncertainty. You cannot hide from it. Embrace it. It can be full of wonderful surprises. You can deal with what is—remember this. Use love as your guide."

There was no denying the meditations were inspirational for me. I felt privileged to receive the teachings my spirit guides shared. It was humbling to have a relationship with spiritual mentors. I was excited to be able to connect with the spirit world, it felt like I had and exclusive insight to the other side.

But occasionally, I questioned my ability to connect with the spirits. Were my meditations genuine or just an overactive imagination on my part? After all, these conversations all took place with my eyes closed and the voices I heard were not audible to anyone else. I needed tangible proof my spirit guides existed. I had read that doubting your abilities was a normal reaction when you are new to the process of crossing over and asking for confirmation from your guides would be welcomed. I decided to ask them for validation.

I contemplated on which guide to help me with my dilemma. Two White Feathers was notorious for proving a point and his advice was always straight forward. On one occasion, he simply warned me to "Watch your back." I thought he was referring to some gossip going around at work, but later that day I slipped on a wet floor and literally hurt my lower back. I quickly learned he was to be taken at his actual word. I elected to give him the job.

Knowing he liked a direct approach, I didn't beat around the bush when I asked him, "Two White Feathers, I need physical proof that you really exist. Can you please show yourself to me? I need validation you are real." He agreed! He instructed me to go into my library (I was still an avid reader), pull down an art book he named, and turn to page 113. I would find my proof there.

As soon as I finished the meditation, I did what he asked. I found the book and flipped to the page he requested. Located on the page was a beautiful painting of two Native American men with a herd of horses.

"Nice painting," I said. "But that's not proof of *you.*"

"Look again." I heard his voice in my head. I scanned the picture a second time. What was I missing? Then I saw it. One of the men had two white feathers dangling from his headdress. WOW. The conformation I was looking for was right in front of me, Two White Feathers. I just received positive proof this was not my imagination; this was for real. I was awestruck. The spiritual connections I had were fact, not fiction. I could trust myself and my meditations and could now move confidently forward. I just wish my guides had given me a heads up on what I was about to encounter next.

THE TRUTH NEVER LEFT ME

CHAPTER THREE

O NE FALL AFTERNOON, I found myself home alone without much to do. With the house nice and quiet, I decided to meditate. The living room was my go-to place to meditate as it had two large windows that illuminated the entire room. It always felt light and airy and if the time of day was just right, you got an extra bonus of warm sunlight shining down on you. I sat on my favorite area of the floor with my back up against the sofa and began the process.

I aligned my energy and said my prayer of protection as usual. My breathing soon relaxed my body enough to get started. I arrived at my lovely scenic spot, but this time, my spirit guides weren't there. Odd—that had never happened before. Standing in their place was a handsome man in his thirties with beautiful brown eyes, brown shoulder-length hair and a beard. His clothing hinted he was from an ancient time as he wore a light-colored tunic made of course cloth that draped down to his knees, a black chord for a belt, and plain leather sandals. He was holding a pewter goblet adorned with rough cut stones.

I had been visited by various spirits before, so I was not surprised in seeing someone new. There was something different about this man I couldn't put my finger on, but his eyes were inviting, and I felt safe with him, so I choose to let him proceed with whatever message he had for me.

"Hello," he said with a smile.

"Hello," I replied.

"Drink this," he said as he handed the chalice to me. "This is the drink of life." I took the cup and drank its contents. It was water, but not like any water I had ever tasted. I can only describe it as the most refreshing and purest water you can imagine. He then handed me a small, round wafer that looked like a cracker.

"Eat this," he said. "This is the bread of my body." Wait. *What?* That phrase sounded vaguely familiar. There was only one person I was aware of that could say anything remotely similar to that. I looked down at the wafer in my hand and kept my eyes lowered as I slowly put it in my mouth. I started to panic. This couldn't possibly be who I thought it could be. Was I really standing in front of almighty Jesus? Jesus! I didn't know what to do. I couldn't lift my eyes to look at him, yet I couldn't just stand there and *not* look at him. My mind went blank. I couldn't process the fact that the most powerful being in the universe, the one and only Son of God just handed me bread of his body. I was scared to death, but knew I had to do something.

I cautiously lifted my head to find him smiling at me with a playful twinkle in his eyes. He knew I knew it was Him, and He found it amusing. As He patiently paused and waited for me to get my bearings, I could feel His all-encompassing love and compassion surround me like a warm hug.

He then gently declared, "I never left you."

I lost it; I had to get out of there as fast as I could. I remember His kind, steady gaze as He watched me backpedal out of the meditation. Safely back in my living room, I tried to fathom what just happened. Jesus! I actually stood before Jesus Christ! He's for real! Jesus is alive and He revealed Himself to me! My mind was racing. I cried. I laughed. He said He never left me! Jesus spoke to me! I was shaking.

I don't know how long I sat there totally dumbfounded; it was a lot to take in. Who was I that Jesus would appear to me? I was no one special. I was just an everyday, average person whose world was small and routine. I hadn't accomplished anything of great worth; I had the same job my entire life and didn't even have a college degree. I was a Nobody. I wasn't even going to church! But Jesus made me feel like I *was* worth something without saying a word. He never stopped loving me, even all those years I had drifted away from Him. *He never left me.* I was overwhelmingly grateful, humbled, and ashamed at the same time. Jesus was real and He loved me. My life was changed in an instant.

I knew I had to tell Bob about the Jesus visit when he got home from work. This wasn't going to be an easy conversation. Even though Bob was used to hearing about my meditations, this one was obviously different. It's not every day you get a visit from Jesus, and I wasn't sure how he was going to handle it. I was still trying to handle it myself.

Bob took the news better than I expected; thankfully, he didn't doubt me. Once the initial shock wore off, we calmly talked it out. We didn't understand why Jesus chose to visit me, but we realized he had a reason for doing so and maybe one day we would discover why. But what were we supposed to do in the meantime? I strongly felt I needed to terminate the meditations. I was done with them. The desire to communicate with the other side left me immediately the moment Jesus showed up. I knew I was dabbling with powerful forces I didn't completely understand, and I was way in over my head. But where did I go from here? I still wanted spiritual guidance and in lieu of current events and could also use some help deciphering the Jesus experience. Bob and I could only come up with one answer—time to get our butts back to church.

In the ten years Bob and I were married, we never went to a church, other than weddings and funerals. We both had gone to church as kids, but as adults, life had gotten busy with other obligations and distractions; practicing our Christian faith wasn't a priority. Looking for a church to attend can be quite a challenge. Bob was raised in the Catholic faith and I was not, so we decided on trying a non-denominational church. It was a compromise we both felt comfortable with. We looked in the phonebook and found a non-denominational church nearby. We didn't know anything about it, but we were soon to find out.

The church was an eyeopener, to say the least. It was huge. We walked into a beautiful sanctuary and I thought, *Nice! I could get used to this place.* The seats were comfy, and the altar was impressive. The service started with a magnificent choir dressed in beautiful burgundy robes. They were very good, and with the words to the hymns on a big screen, we sang along. When the music stopped, I noticed some of the parishioners were still humming along. Not really humming, but chanting, with their arms stretched out and heads tilted back. I had never seen churchgoers act that way.

All of a sudden, a man abruptly stood up from the audience and yelled out something I didn't recognize as English. Then another man shot up out of his seat and did the same. What in the world was going on here? What kind of church was *this*? I didn't wait around to find out.

I nudged Bob and said, "Come on, we're out of here." Up and out we went; we didn't even stay for the sermon. I apologized to God for walking out of His church, but when something doesn't feel right, it probably isn't, and I was going to trust my instincts on this one.

I needed to find a church that felt a little more familiar. I remembered the Baptist church I attended with my Aunt Marsha, so I searched the internet and found an Independent Baptist church nearby. I knew the Bible would be taught there, hopefully without the dramatics I didn't understand. Bob and I drove up for Sunday morning services and found a quaint, red brick church with a traditional white steeple on top. Once inside, we were greeted by more than one friendly person. This place wasn't trying to be a megachurch; you could feel the sense of community here. This time we stayed for the sermon and liked the pastor's message.

We started attending, sporadically at first, but I was drawn in by the biblical teachings and before long we were regular pew warmers. I was learning about the Jesus who revealed Himself to me and I loved it. When I read the Bible as a youngster, I occasionally felt Jesus was disappointed with me and I heard frustration in his words when he taught. But after His visit, I was able to put His kind and humble voice to the written Word and it changed my perspective entirely. Jesus loves us unconditionally, with all our sins and faults. He's our number one fan, always in our corner, ready to encourage and comfort us. He's patient and compassionate, while also strong and unwavering. I was thankful for this new insight; because of it I wanted to begin a relationship with Jesus. I no longer felt judged by God, just incredibly loved.

I enjoyed the Sunday morning sermons, but during the services my mind would often drift back to the Jesus visit. *I never left you.* Did it really happen? I was second guessing myself again. The experience felt real enough. It changed my life, that was for sure, but did I subconsciously make it all up? The question haunted me. I needed validation, but where was I going to find it? If you go around telling people you've seen Jesus, they have a tendency to think you're a little crazy. The only person I even told about it was Bob. I wasn't comfortable sharing my encounter with the pastor. We were on friendly terms, but I didn't think he knew me well enough to realize I wasn't a total wackadoodle. Once again, I turned to books for an answer.

I researched true life accounts of Jesus visits with everyday folks like me. I read amazing testimonies of various visions, dreams and actual unexpected appearances. Jesus has shown Himself to numerous people for all sorts of reasons, from healing to comforting to salvation. It was reassuring to know I wasn't the only one who had witnessed Jesus up close and personal. I appreciated these stories, but they didn't give me the validation I was looking for.

I played with the idea of consulting a psychic on the issue. I knew a spiritualist who claimed to be a Christian, if anyone could confirm my Jesus experience, it was probably her. I battled back and forth—should I go, should I not. I was aware the church would frown on it, but I needed answers. I wanted to know if a "professional" could see my experience with help from the other side. I was torn between what the Bible was teaching me about God's dislike of mediums and what I was comfortable with. What to do. I really wanted validation on my Jesus visit. Curiosity killed the cat; I called and made an appointment.

On the afternoon of my reading, I arrived at the psychic's house and was ushered upstairs to a tiny room decorated with paintings of Jesus and angels. Meredith was a woman in her late sixties with blonde hair and a warm, friendly smile. She graciously asked me to take a seat in a comfortable chair across from her. I was so excited. Please God, let her see my Jesus experience. I wasn't going to mention my encounter; I didn't want to tip my hand and have her expand on any information I gave her. She started the reading with a prayer.

Good so far. She then gave me personal messages from many of my deceased family members, whom she was able to accurately identify by name. I had greetings from my Aunt Marsha, my Grandpa and even Bob's Grandma who thanked me for putting a picture of our dog in her casket (she loved our dog and always volunteered to puppy sit when we went on vacation). The reading was captivating, but not what I wanted to hear.

Then she said, "I'm seeing something I've never seen before." Now, I'm on the edge of my seat. "You have a special spirit guide sent to you," she continued. "His mission is specifically to help you write books. He will dictate messages to you, which you will then take and make your own. I see many books around you. In all my years of doing readings, I've never seen this."

Interesting, but not the message I was hoping for. I was disappointed; she didn't mention Jesus. However, I was intrigued by what she did relay. Maybe this was the answer to another one of my unresolved questions: what was my purpose in life? Have you ever thought about why you were put on this Earth? I did. All the time. I didn't know what my purpose was, and it drove me crazy. I had read many books on the subject (what a surprise) but could never figure it out. I always felt I was meant to do something significant, but just what that would be always eluded me.

Maybe this was what I was supposed to accomplish in life—write books! I liked the idea as writing was on my bucket list. I enjoyed English in high school and even took a few poetry classes on the internet. The psychic's message gave me something new to contemplate. I didn't receive the validation I was looking for, but did walk away with a fresh, new outlook on what the future possibly held for me.

The only problem with my newfound direction was I

would have to perform spiritual meditations again and I was apprehensive. I had vowed to stop doing them after seeing Jesus. I knew I would be treading in dangerous waters, but there was a new spirit guide waiting for me. We had books to write. I had a purpose. Maybe Jesus had something to do with it—I didn't know. The psychic said she was a Christian, could I trust her message? She knew my relatives by name and told me things no one else knew about; that was true. So, I trusted the rest of it to be true too. After months of deliberation, I made a decision. It was time to meet this new spirit guide.

Once again, I found myself sitting on the living room floor preparing to meditate. It had been a long time since I had contacted the other side and it felt strange to be attempting this again. I aligned my chakras, said a prayer of protection, and regulated my breathing. It was surprising how quickly my body fell into the rhythm of the relaxation required to crossover. I proceeded to my familiar spiritual place.

Sister Mary and Two White Feathers were standing on our grassy hilltop, ready to welcome me. It was like a family reunion; they were happy to see me, and I them. After the initial hugs and good-to-see-you's, I got right down to the matter at hand.

"So, I hear I have a guide that wants to help me write books. Is that true?" I asked them.

Sister Mary answered, "Yes! Would you like to meet him?" I still wasn't sure. Was I supposed to be doing this? The Bible instructs us not to contact spirits and I knew I could be getting myself into trouble. I hesitated, like a little kid at the edge of a swimming pool needing to be coaxed to jump in. There was just something about this whole thing that didn't feel quite right. My mind kept going back to I never left you. Jesus loved me, and I didn't want to disappoint him by doing something He might not be on board with.

"Is Jesus okay with this?" I asked. No sooner than I got the words out, there was a blinding flash of light and Jesus was instantly at my side. Instinctively, I fell to the ground on my face at his feet. I was in the presence of the Lord and this time I knew it. My spirit guides simultaneously vanished; it was just Jesus and me. I started crying. I don't even know why I was crying—the tears just came. My emotions and thoughts were running faster than I could keep up with them. In the middle of it all, I remember feeling Jesus' overpowering love; it was an energy that enveloped everything. There was no judgement, I was allowed to be my genuine self and did so without thinking.

I thought of my business, which was currently experiencing a difficult period and I didn't know if we were going to recover or not. The economy had taken a turn for the worse and we were hit hard. I was devastated to think I could lose the business my family started. The studio had always been part of my life and it was the only financial security I had ever known. I didn't know how to do anything else. I spent many sleepless nights worrying over our finances and our future. Without even realizing what I was saying, I just blurted out to Jesus, "Is my business going to be okay? I'm so worried!"

Jesus tentatively bent down, gently took me by the elbow and lifted me up. I remember he wore a beautiful, full-length white gown. It was both glorious and soothing to look at.

"Haven't I always taken care of you?" He replied. His words were tender, patient and compassionate. He paused for a moment, and then smiling with that familiar glint in his eye, He said, "It's time to do *my* work." And in the blink of an eye, He was gone as quickly as He appeared.

ENLIGHTENED

CHAPTER FOUR

ONCE AGAIN, I was caught off guard by the unexpected presence of Jesus. This time I was not afraid of Him, overwhelmed—but not afraid. Since His first visit, there wasn't a day that went by that I didn't think about Him or his personal message for me, *I never left you.* I can't tell you how many times I played His words over in my head; it was a record I couldn't begin to wear out. Now, I've just been blessed with a second visit. Incredible. Jesus was so patient with me; I've never felt so loved as in his presence.

"Haven't I always taken care of you?" He asked me. Of course, He had. I just never realized the vastness of His love until now. When I look back on all the sticky situations I had gotten myself into over the years, and even the ones I accidentally fell into, I survived every one of them. It wasn't the Universe or fate that delivered me, it was Jesus. He was quietly behind the scenes protecting and providing for me my entire life and I was oblivious. Once I understood how much He had done for me, I felt like an idiot, a very grateful idiot, but an idiot just the same. Jesus is amazing. He didn't scold me or criticize me when He had the chance; He simply made me feel loved.

I was now able to quit stressing over the possibility of my business crashing. Sure, I was aware that it still could, but I was done losing sleep over it. I knew in my heart from that day forward, if the studio was to go belly up, we would be okay. My security was no longer placed in earning money or gaining material possessions, but in trusting God to provide for all my needs. He always had and I knew He always would. I was like the birds Jesus spoke of in the Bible that didn't sow or reap, yet our Heavenly Father feeds them. God loves the insignificant sparrows enough to provide for them and we mean so much more to Him than the birds. We are not to worry about these things, He knows our needs and if we seek Him first, He will take care of us.

It was an awesome relief to know that God had my future in his hands. How much time had I spent needlessly worrying over money and if I would have enough of it? I put those fears behind me. I would still do my part by being financially responsible, but Jesus helped me understand there's so much more in His plan for us than having us worry about material things. He's got it covered.

During the meditation, Jesus said it was time to do his work. I was puzzled. What work? What was He talking about? I didn't have a clue. Was I supposed to sell my business and become a missionary? That didn't feel right; I definitely wasn't missionary material. I didn't have the adventurous personality needed for that type of work. Did His mission for me involve my spirit guides? I didn't think so. They took off every time Jesus appeared. I was back to the same old question: what was my purpose? Now here I was, freshly given an assignment from Jesus Himself and in my never-ending stupidity, couldn't figure out what it was.

I was reluctant to share my Jesus encounters with anyone other than Bob and my parents, so asking for advice, even from the pastor, still wasn't an option for me. I searched the Bible and read about good works. As Christians, we were supposed to recognize the needs of others and help the less fortunate such as orphans, widows and the poor. I thought if I got involved in a charitable activity, it would be considered doing God's work. Doing *something* was better than doing nothing. So, until God let me know for sure what I was supposed to do, I thought volunteering would be a good place to start. I didn't know what else to do, so Bob and I decided to volunteer at a local foodbank.

We enjoyed our time at the food pantry. It was a bustling place as the need for food in our community was surprisingly great. The staff was friendly, and they appreciated our help since they were always shorthanded. But the work was physical, and my abilities were limited because I was living with chronic backpain. All the years of photo retouching at the studio had taken its toll and I was dealing with three herniated disks. I had tried everything short of surgery to alleviate the pain, including physical therapy, chiropractors, shots, and even acupuncture. There were days my body just wouldn't cooperate, and we finally had to quit volunteering at the foodbank. I was disappointed but realized God must have other plans for me.

As opportunities arose at the church, I would volunteer where I could, but I didn't feel like I was accomplishing what Jesus had intended for me. I wanted to be obedient but didn't have a clear direction as to what His work for me was. It was very aggravating. Once again, I was searching for answers on my own without much success. I felt like I was letting God down. If Jesus had only told me specifically what He wanted me to do, I could get started on it. I prayed about it. I even asked for a sign—anything. I got silence. This frustration went on for months. Then one day, I had an idea.

During my last two meditations, Jesus had appeared unexpectedly. What if I prayed and asked Him if He would show up *intentionally*? We could get this business of my purpose out of the way and I could begin serving Him wholeheartedly. What was the worst that could happen? He would stand me up and I would be left with my mission still a mystery. I earnestly prayed on my knees, then with hopeful expectations, set aside a day and time to meditate with the Lord. I innocently thought if I made an actual date with Jesus, my odds would be better that He would keep the appointment.

It was a Monday afternoon, my normal day off. Bob was at work and I was home alone. I hadn't meditated since the last Jesus appearance, and I was excited to give this a try. This meditation was going to be different from my other sessions; I wasn't going to visit my usual spiritual meeting place. No spirit guides needed today, this was more of a prayer with just Jesus and me. I would welcome any type of visitation from the Lord: a voice, a sign - anything.

Once I settled in, I began my prayer. "Jesus," I said. "Thank you for all the blessings you've given me. Thank you for dying on that cross and saving me. Thank you for forgiving my sins and giving me eternal life. I am truly grateful. But today Lord, I need your help. I want to do your work, but I don't know what it is. I need your wisdom and guidance. Please help me. Please tell me what it is you want me to do. Amen." Pause. Nothing. I kept my eyes closed, continued with my breathing, and waited. Then I felt it.

A warm, all-encompassing love moved through my entire body and the next thing I know, Jesus was sitting in front of me dressed in the same white, full-length gown He wore before. It was beautiful. He was beautiful! He smiled at me while holding a tiny, round seed between His finger and thumb. I immediately smiled back, totally astounded. Jesus actually showed up! I just sat in awe across from Him. It was so wonderful to be near Him, the words just can't express it.

Jesus directed my attention towards the seed. "Love is like

a mustard seed," He said as He placed the seed in the palm of His open hand. "When you water it…" He paused and wiggled His fingers over the seed. I watched in amazement as raindrops fell from His fingertips onto the seed. "…it grows into a beautiful tree that houses much." The mustard seed then burst into a flourishing miniature tree with tiny birds circling and landing in its branches. It was like a hologram in the palm of His hand. I looked up at Jesus. He was beaming with a huge grin on his face. This was fun for Him and He enjoyed sharing this message with me.

Now it's a strange thing, but when you are in the presence of the Lord, you feel free to be the person you *are,* not the person you're supposed to be. God loves our personalities, complete with all our flaws and shortcomings. When I reflect back on how I acted in front of Jesus I'm embarrassed. But I am who I am, and it was what it was.

My mind was so intensely focused on what Jesus' mission was for me, I was annoyed that He would show me something that had no relevancy with my purpose. "That's nice," I said. Jesus just shared an incredible miracle with me, and I reply with *That's nice.* What an idiot—and it got worse. I then bluntly demand, "But what's my purpose?" Patience was obviously not one of my virtues.

Jesus chuckled and that delightful twinkle returned to his eyes. He loves us more than we can imagine, even when we act like children who insist on having our own way.

Jesus looked at me for a moment then with a smile, answered, "Teach and inspire," and in an instant He was gone.

I was ecstatic! I finally got an answer! Jesus revealed his plan for me: I was to teach and inspire. But there was more to his message than the words He spoke. Let me explain. When I was in His presence, I felt messages as well as heard them.

I don't know if Jesus gave them to me telepathically or how I received them, but I sensed His intentions without being told.

When Jesus looked at me, there was overwhelming sense of relief that I didn't have to worry about fulfilling my purpose any longer. Not because He had just told me to teach and inspire, but because as a child of God, *my* purpose wasn't up to *me* to fulfill, it was *God's*. God had it all worked out. Now that I belonged to Him, He would use me when and how He saw fit. I just had to be ready to serve Him and be open to the opportunities He placed in my path. I had to rest in Him and let Him lead me. God would show me what to do when the time was right for His purpose and His glory.

The question of my purpose was no longer a mystery to figure out. I didn't have to stress over all the details of completing His mission for me. It was a remarkable insight and I was truly grateful for it. It really took the pressure off. Another inner struggle crossed off the list, thank you, Jesus.

However, I didn't understand why Jesus shared the mustard seed analogy with me. It was an unforgettable illustration for sure, but I didn't grasp why He chose *that* example to show me. I felt He was trying to teach me something other than the obvious message and I was missing it. Did I need to work on my capacity to love? Probably, it's an issue we all could use a little improvement on. I'm sure one day, with His help, I'd figure it out.

I was beginning to see a pattern with Jesus. He likes us to contemplate on His spoken word. Jesus is obviously very capable of plainly teaching us what He wants us to learn, but I think He enjoys planting a tiny seed in us and watching it grow. It gives Him joy when our eyes are finally opened, and we discover the truth in His life changing messages. I believe that's one of the reasons He taught in parables or answered a question with a question. He wasn't being arrogant; He was giving us opportunities to meditate on His words and receive His blessings as we put our focus on Him. What a brilliant teacher our Savior is.

I also noticed another pattern with my meditations. Whenever Jesus appeared, my spirit guides would immediately leave. I didn't understand why. If you had the opportunity to be in the presence of the Lord, why wouldn't you? Was it out of respect? Were there rules on the other side I wasn't aware of? I didn't get it. Then one morning, I received a shocking answer.

I was driving to work, half-heartedly listening to the radio. I had dialed in a Christian station and the DJs were carrying on a conversation during their morning show. Someone mentioned New Age Believers and that caught my attention. I turned up the volume. A woman had called in to share that she had converted from New Age to Christianity and was grateful to be saved. The DJs applauded her, and one made a comment that New Age Beliefs were of the devil. *How could that be*, I thought. My spirit guides had nothing but positive messages filled with love and harmony. There was nothing evil in anything they taught me; I would have stopped the meditations immediately if there were.

It was the next comment that spun my head around. I only caught the last part of it, "...and the Devil will flee in the presence of Jesus," one of the DJs said. What?! I almost had to pull the car over; the statement hit me like a ton of bricks. *My spirit guides had fled* each time Jesus arrived. I was horrified. Could it be true? Could my beloved spirit guides actually be demons working with Satan? But why? It didn't make any sense. Later that day, I turned to the Bible for clarification and found it in 1 John 4:1-3:

"Beloved, do not believe every spirit, but test the spirits, whether they are of God; because many false prophets have gone out into the world. By this you know the Spirit of God: Every spirit that confesses that Jesus Christ has come in the flesh is of God, and every spirit that does not confess that Jesus Christ has come in the flesh is not of God. And this is the Spirit of the Antichrist, which you have heard was coming, and is now already in the world."

I looked back through all the notes I had taken during my spiritual meditations and discovered that my spirit guides had never once mentioned Jesus. Not one time. I was floored. I was so caught up in what I was experiencing with my guides, I never noticed the absence of Jesus in any of their teachings. In all the time I spent meditating, I never questioned the source behind the information I was receiving. I naively thought because their messages were based in love, my guides were from Heaven. I couldn't have been more wrong.

Now, I understand a lot of people don't believe in the Devil. I get it—he's a scary guy to think about. But Jesus is for real and He spoke of the Devil, so, sorry, that makes Satan real too. I did some research and found that the devil was once an angel named Lucifer who, through his own arrogance and jealousy, started a revolt against God and was cast out of Heaven with a group of angels who sided with him. The more I read about what the Bible had to say about the devil, the more I realized how duped I had really been, for it reveals in 2 Corinthians 11:14 "And no wonder! For Satan himself transforms himself into an angel of light."

Why would Satan do that? Simple, Satan hates us. He's a liar that will use any means possible to lure us away from Jesus, even disguise himself as an angel of light with beautiful messages of love and being one with the universe, because he knows without Jesus we are lost souls.

Jesus taught us, "I am the way, the truth, and the life. No one comes to the Father except through Me," John 14:6. If we think we can obtain Heaven on our own, without Jesus, then Satan has us right where he wants us—in his demonic grasp.

For all of you who are intrigued with psychics, or are practicing the metaphysical or New Age spirituality, please don't make the same mistake I did. Test the source of the knowledge you are receiving. Where is it really coming from? I can sincerely tell you this: if Jesus isn't in it, stay away from it. I can't make it any plainer than that. Playing with the spirit world isn't a harmless game, it's a gamble with your soul and you don't want to take a risk where the stakes are so high—there's just too much to lose. "Be sober, be vigilant; because your adversary the devil walks about like a roaring lion, seeking whom he may devour," 1 Peter 5:8.

When I think about how close I was to falling into the devil's snare, it makes me sick to my stomach. Looking back at my psychic reading with Meredith, of course she didn't see my Jesus experience, her guides weren't going to speak His name. Of course, my new "spirit guide" would dictate *his* messages to me—messages that were meant to lure myself and others away from the Lord. Satan almost had me as a willing participant to do his bidding. It all made horrible, gut-wrenching sense.

I can't thank Jesus enough for literally stepping in and saving me. His gracious appearances in my meditations had more intention than just a miraculous visit. My innocent road to enlightenment was a hidden pathway to Hell and I was blindly bumbling along. I had no idea. My eyes were fully opened on that morning drive to work. Jesus had never left me, and I was never going to leave him again. Ever.

I thought about all the books I had read about the other side, there was a mountain of them. I went into my library, found every book I had on the metaphysical, and threw them all out. Garbage. I thought about the countless other people that had read the same books I had and were unsuspectedly walking down the same path, thinking they too were being enlightened. It was tragic; the devil was working on an enormous scale and was deceptively leading so many away from Jesus and our real Heavenly home.

In the Bible, God sternly warns us in Deuteronomy 18:10-12:

"There shall not be found among you anyone who makes his son or his daughter pass through the fire, or one who practices witchcraft, or a soothsayer, or one who interprets omens, or a sorcerer, or one who conjures spells, or a medium, or a spiritist, or one who calls up the dead. For all who do these things are an abomination to the Lord, and because of these abominations the Lord your God drives them out from before you."

I thank God every day for driving them away from *me*. God instructs us to stay away from these things, not because they aren't real (I know firsthand they are *very* real), but because God loves us and knows that the evil deception of Satan and his demons are often behind them. How many lives have been ruined and souls lost because of innocent involvements with the occult or the metaphysical? I was almost a victim myself. There's so much more to the other side than we can comprehend, trust God when he tries to protect you from it.

This was a huge turning point in my walk with Christ. I thought I was on a journey of enlightenment, a mission in search of the truth. The fact that Jesus would personally protect me from my own, ignorant downfall was extremely humbling. He was the only truth I ever needed. I clung to the words written in James 4:7-8: "Therefore submit to God. Resist the devil and he will flee from you. Draw near to God and He will draw near to you…"

This scriptural passage really reflected my personal relationship with Jesus—and His relationship with me. My meditations with Him were just the beginning. Jesus was going to draw nearer to me in ways I never expected.

HE IS THE POTTER

CHAPTER FIVE

A WHILE AGO, I had asked Jesus to come into my life, forgive me of my sins and make Heaven my home, and by doing so, I was saved, and my eternal future was secured. Now I was building a closer relationship with Him by praying more, reading the Bible, and going to church. I recently asked the Lord to show me where I could make personal improvements and to mold me into a better person. Not because I needed to change who I was in order to be saved, with God's grace we're automatically saved when we accept Jesus, but I wanted to be a better version of me because I love Him. When you ask God to help you with something, He's always up for the challenge. The only problem is that we're not always up for his methods. God would mold me, alright, I just had one idea in mind, and He had quite another.

Bob and I were living life fairly well, by now we were in our late forties. We had good incomes and were able to pay our bills and put money aside for retirement. Sure, there were ups and downs, but we were pretty steady financially. We weren't big spenders with designer clothes or the latest gadgets and our idea of dinner out was at the local diner, not an expensive steak house. We were living within our means and it was working for us. We only had one spending vice—we liked casinos.

I guess it started on our Honeymoon. We took a Caribbean

cruise and there was a casino on the ship. We ventured in and tried our luck at the slot machines. With all the flashing lights and the sounds of the machines going off, it was an exciting place to be. It was kind of like fishing—you threw twenty bucks in a machine and hit the play button until you caught something. Sometimes, you had something on the line and sometimes the line broke. We won a little money and had a good time in the process.

When we got home, we realized we liked playing slot machines for entertainment. We didn't have any casinos near us, so we decided our next vacation would include gambling. Over the years, we hit a lot of destination casinos from the Bahamas, Las Vegas, and Atlantic City, to even small towns in Colorado and Arizona. Casinos were becoming part of our trips, and we didn't think much of it.

Things changed when they built a huge casino across the Canadian border in Windsor, Ontario. This was the big, new attraction in our area, and everyone was trying their luck there, including us. Now, we were going to Canada with friends and family for a casual night out of dinner and gaming.

It didn't take long for Detroit to follow suit and before we knew it, casinos were popping up in the Motor City. This was great news for us as we no longer had to wait in lines to exchange our currency or pay the toll to cross over to Canada and back. We now had beautiful Vegas-style casinos complete with restaurants, hotels, and concert venues forty minutes away from home. Like many of our friends, we became regulars. The casinos offered reward cards that you inserted in the slot machine while you played, and you could earn comps for their food or a night's stay. We took advantage of the rewards and often ate at their buffets for free.

For Bob and me, it was entertainment with the possibility of getting our money back. We knew the odds were stacked against us at winning a big jackpot, but it was something fun to do and we were responsible about how much money we spent. We only took what we budgeted for and when the money ran out, we went home, not to the ATM machine. The only problem was, we were going to the casino more often than we should have.

Soon after I purchased the photography studio from my parents, Bob did likewise and bought the finish carpentry business from his folks. Eight years after he did so, the housing market bottomed out and many people lost their homes. Builders quit paying their contractors, and Bob, being one of them, lost thousands. Devastated, he had no choice but to close up shop. When you lose your income as a business owner, unemployment doesn't go very far, he was given eight weeks of benefits. With the job market also down, his prospects for finding work were limited. It just so happened that we had an opening at the studio for a sales position, so he came on board. Now Bob and I were working the same hours, which gave us the same days off, which meant more available time to spend at the casino.

We would often go to church on Sunday and the casino on Monday. I was starting to feel that maybe this wasn't such a good idea. Bob and I were spending more time in the Baptist church and our casino activities didn't line up with the rest of our lives. We were making friends at church, but keeping our gambling hidden from them. I felt like I was living a lie. I realized God was nudging me to give up gambling and do something more constructive with my time and money.

Bob had grown up in the Catholic Church and gambling was not an issue for him, they often had casino nights as fundraisers at the church. When we were dating, Bob took me one evening to a church sponsored Vegas tent. It was the first time I had ever played blackjack and to my surprise, the priest was the dealer who actually helped me learn the rules of the game! I thought for sure that lightning was going to strike me down that night. Many of Bob's family were visiting the casinos on a regular basis and no one seemed to question it. But God had a different plan for my life, and He wasn't giving up on me. That little voice that said stop going to the casinos was getting louder.

Being a creature of the flesh, I didn't want to give up my casino fun. I started justifying it with all sorts of excuses. I told myself this wasn't really gambling, it was entertainment. Gambling meant you were taking a risk you couldn't afford. We never played with money earmarked for bills, it was money set aside for a good time. Some people spent money on season sports tickets or expensive vacations, we didn't; we went to the casino for amusement. We weren't hurting anyone else or neglecting any of our responsibilities, we just liked to play slot machines. I had a whole list of reasons why we should be able to continue going to the casino. God wasn't buying any of it.

I was starting to feel His work on my heart even more. The weekend would roll around and I wanted to go to the casino but knew we shouldn't. I would tell myself it was only for a couple hours and we'd get back home before anyone knew we were gone. Even though God was prompting me otherwise, I would always give in to the temptation and downtown we'd go. On the drive home, I was relieved the gambling episode was over and would promise God this would be the last time, to please forgive me, as I would now get serious and stop going to the casino. Then the next weekend would roll around and I would do it all over again. It was a vicious cycle. I knew my behavior was wrong, but I couldn't stop myself. It wasn't even about the money, but the casinos had their grip on me, and I couldn't break free.

I looked to the church for help. Oh, I didn't actually talk to anyone about my problem, but I waited for the Pastor to address the issue of gambling in a sermon. He never did. I wished he had, but our church focused on God's salvation, love, grace, and how to let Him be a part of your life; not nitpicking on all your sins. I would often hear sermons on TV about staying away from adultery, alcohol, or drugs—but never heard a sermon on gambling. Trust me, I was listening.

Casinos are a grey area, like anything else that's legal—just because you can doesn't mean you should. We live in a fallen world where many things that are acceptable to man aren't acceptable to God. They weren't when God first created man and they still aren't today. The world may change but God never does, and while He hates the sin, thank goodness He still loves the sinner. I knew Jesus loved me, but the lifestyle I was living was a sin.

I prayed about it all the time. I felt I was seriously letting God down. Jesus thought enough of me to visit me on three separate occasions, and I didn't have enough will power to give up the casinos for Him. I was ashamed, and I also felt He was growing impatient with me. I had been battling with this issue for a couple of years and couldn't end it. What had started out as innocent fun so long ago was now turning into a nightmare. I was having anxiety over it and was trying to control this monster on my own, without much luck.

After another Monday afternoon at the casino, I was completely exhausted from the inner struggle. I had hit rock bottom. When we got home, I crept into our bedroom, flung myself across the bed and started to cry. I don't know if you've ever been in a low, dark place like that, but when you realize your problems are bigger than you are and you don't know how you're going to get over them, your emotions become pretty raw. I was desperate.

I started confessing to God, "I'm so sorry, Lord. I know I've let you down. I keep saying I'm going to stop gambling and I don't. I don't know how I'm going to turn this around; I can't do it without you. I've tried on my own and I don't know what else to do. I don't know *anything*. All I know is that I love you." At this point, I was sobbing.

Then I heard a quiet, still voice that said, "Look up."

I raised my head and opened my eyes. To my disbelief, I looked up and saw Jesus standing outside my bedroom window! He was glowing and his beautiful white gown was the brightest white I had ever seen. He had one hand over His heart and the other hand was slightly reached out with His palm facing me. He looked at me compassionately and without moving his lips, said, "That's all you need to know. Let me do the rest." And in a split second, He was gone.

This was no meditation. My eyes were wide open, and I saw Jesus plain as day! I was awestruck. Jesus came to me again and this time there was no doubt it was for real! There was no doubt *He* was for real. With the meditations, I always had a little doubt my experiences might be my creative imagination, but this was a different experience entirely and, in that instant, all skepticism left me.

I felt His magnificent love once again and total relief; my struggle was finally going to be over. I was elated. I had reached out to God with honest, unabashed raw emotion and He heard me. Help was here. He *was* here. I was going to be okay. Jesus is astounding. He'll pick us up when we're at our lowest and lead us to a better place every time, if we let Him. Jesus said in John 14:27: "Peace I leave with you, My peace I give to you; not as the world gives, do I give to you. Let not your heart be troubled, neither let it be afraid." The anxiety I had over gambling left me instantly.

Did my behavior change instantly? No, not immediately,

but it did change. Jesus said, "Let me do the rest", and I trusted him to fight this battle for me. And He did. Week by week, He took away the strong desire I had to go to the casino. I wasn't struggling with the emotional rollercoaster of temptation anymore. On the rare occasion when we went with friends, my attitude was entirely changed. The casinos had lost their exciting appeal. I felt like they were luring people in with the unrealistic hope of winning a fortune, only to take their money in the process. I didn't want to support an industry that had ruined people's lives in order to make a profit; they had taken enough of my time and money. Casinos were a total waste of time for me now, and I had Jesus to thank for that. My addiction was over.

I think deep down we all know when we're doing something we shouldn't. God prompts us with that little voice because He loves us and wants a better life for us. If you are dealing with unresolved, obvious sin, consider putting it in God's hands and let Him help you with it. Going through a behavioral struggle with God may get uncomfortable, but it always turns out for our better good when we finally submit to Him and let Him work in our lives.

I now had a new desire. I wanted to spend my time doing things that would please God because I wanted to give back to Him in some way for all He had done for me. So instead of running downtown to the casinos on Mondays, I began volunteering in the church office. I learned a lot about what goes on behind the scenes in a busy church and how much help is really required to get things done. It was fun to be involved. I was making friends with the church staff while being a blessing in God's house. It felt good to contribute to a cause bigger than myself and be helpful to others.

I also started painting for God. I always had an interest in art, so instead of foolishly spending my money at the slot machines, I was now purchasing canvases and paint to create large, colorful abstracts with Christian themes. I even opened a store on the internet where I could share my art and love for Jesus. I was expressing my love for God in my own, creative way and it felt great.

When I had asked God to mold me, I thought He would show me the little things I could do to improve myself—like becoming more patient or less critical. I had no idea He was going to zero in on the big stuff. But I'm glad He did. Asking God to shape me into a better person was a big step in being obedient to Him and I don't regret it. My life is so much more fulfilling because I submitted to Him and with His help, changed my ways. Removing my obvious sin has allowed me to become closer to God and take our relationship even farther.

God is the potter and He is always willing to shape us into something better. Even though it might take spinning us around and putting us through the fire, it's worth the effort to be transformed from a muddy lump of clay into a beautiful piece of pottery ready to be used for God's purpose.

THE GOOD SHEPHERD

CHAPTER SIX

ONCE I GAVE up the gambling, my relationship with Jesus began to soar. Since seeing Him outside my window, any residual doubts I had about Him being real were completely gone and with my sin being removed, I felt closer to Him. Experiences started to happen on a more frequent basis. I began to hear His voice in ways I never expected.

The first time it happened, I was blown away. I was home on a Saturday afternoon catching up on housework and laundry. Bob was at a buddy's house and I turned on the TV to have some background noise keep me company. I had finished folding a load of whites and was carrying them through the living room on the way to the bedroom to put them away. I paused in front of the TV for a moment because it visually grabbed my attention.

A college football game was about to start, and the cameras were scanning the crowds. The entire stadium was chanting for the home team to come out of the locker room and the place was pulsating with yellow pompoms held by the cheering fans. There were thousands of people chanting and waving in unison, almost worshipping these football players. It was an eerie spectacle to watch.

The scene really affected me and, without even thinking, I just said out loud, "Why can't they do that for *You, Lord?*"

To my surprise, I heard His voice reply, "In Heaven, they do." I almost dropped my laundry! I thought I was absentmindedly talking to myself. I never expected Jesus would answer my question, but with Jesus, I was learning to expect the unexpected. I loved the surprise; it was like getting flowers for no special reason—just because. His response made me smile. What a wonderful thought to visualize the vast multitudes in Heaven cheering for Jesus. I was delighted to hear Him say it—He deserves an eternity of our praise.

It was the first time I really understood that Jesus is with us all the time. We truly are never alone in this life when we let Jesus into our hearts. It's a very comforting thought. It's also a little amusing to think of how many people would change their behavior if they realized that Jesus was in the room. If they only knew...

On another occasion when Jesus spoke to me, He had a more personal message to deliver. I was going through a phase of feeling distant from God. I knew God was with me, for He tells us in Hebrews 13:5 "...I will never leave you nor forsake you." But I just wasn't feeling Him. I knew the distance I was feeling was my fault, not God's. It was during our busy season at work, and with my other obligations at home and with family, I was preoccupied with worldly things. When I had a spare moment, I spent it on me, not on my relationship with God. I hadn't read my Bible for a couple weeks and was feeling disconnected.

I remembered the Bible verse in Psalm 46:10 "Be still, and know that I *am* God", and thought to myself, good idea. It's so easy to get distracted from all the noise in our lives with our computers, television, radio, and cellphones. Combine that with all the activities that make up our day, and it's easy for God to get lost in the shuffle. I decided to set aside some quiet time to be still and just be in the presence of the Lord.

On that particular afternoon, I went into the bedroom where I knew I wouldn't be disturbed, closed the door and began to pray. I started by thanking God for what I was grateful for. Next, I apologized to Jesus about my drifting, "Jesus, I'm sorry I haven't been spending time with you. I feel like you're far away and I need you near me. I miss you and I want to feel you in my life again. Please forgive me. How can I make this better?" I paused for a moment, I just wanted to be still and feel Him. I took a few minutes to sit quietly with my eyes closed and feel my breathing, in and out like waves of water washing up on a shore.

I sensed that familiar warmth come over me and once again, heard Jesus' soothing voice, "Do you love Me?"

I was crushed. That's never a question you want to have Jesus ask you. I was heartbroken to think that He would question my love for Him. I started to cry. I didn't realize how important our love is to Jesus. I always thought that I was an insignificant player in the big scheme of things, after all Jesus has the whole world and Heaven to love Him, and I was just one person that wouldn't even be missed. I didn't think I was important enough for Jesus to care if I loved Him or not- but He does care. It's very important to Him that each and every one of us love Him back.

All I could muster to say through my tears was, "Yes, Lord."

"Do you hear My voice?" He continued.

"Yes, Lord."

"Then be my lamb. Be my lamb."

There was nothing but love in His voice. I was once again overwhelmed. The tears just poured out; it was very humbling. Now, when Jesus told me to be His lamb, He wasn't calling me by a random pet name, He had another purpose in mind. For Jesus says in John 10:14-15 "I am the good shepherd; and I know My sheep and am known by My own. As the Father

knows Me, even so I know the Father; and I lay down My life
for the sheep". He continues in John 10:27-28 "My sheep hear
My voice, and I know them, and they follow Me. And I give
them eternal life, and they shall never perish; neither shall
anyone snatch them out of My hand."

Jesus considered me one of His own—I was one of His
sheep! I was more than happy to be part of His flock and under
His guidance; there was no place I'd rather be. It was a blessing
to hear His words once again. Jesus wanted me to follow Him
and He was gently reminding me to put Him first. That's what
He wants from all of us. It was a life changing message.

I thought of how Jesus' perfect love for us is described in
Psalm 23:

The Lord is my shepherd;
I shall not want.
He makes me to lie down in green pastures;
He leads me beside the still waters.
He restores my soul;
He leads me in the paths of righteousness
For His name's sake.
Yea, though I walk through the valley of the shadow of
death,
I will fear no evil;
For You are with me;
Your rod and Your staff, they comfort me.
You prepare a table before me in the presence of my
enemies;
You anoint my head with oil;
My cup runs over.
Surely goodness and mercy shall follow me
All the days of my life;
And I will dwell in the house of the Lord Forever.

Who wouldn't want to follow the Good Shepherd who leads us to green pastures, restores our souls when we're hurting, protects us from evil, anoints us with blessings, gives us mercy, and wants us to dwell with Him forever? Do I love Him? With everything I've got.

MAKING CONTACT

CHAPTER SEVEN

WHEN I BEGAN my mission for the truth so long ago, I found myself on a journey that led me down a wrong path. I wanted to experience the spirit world and all its wonders. I got into big trouble because I didn't consider the source of my experiences and was playing with demonic fire. Thanks to Jesus, I didn't get burned. I now understand that both good and evil reside on the other side and to be obedient when God tells us to stay away from these things. Now days, I don't dabble with the spirits, but I still have Heavenly experiences, but with God and only God.

I was discovering that I was not the only Christian that heard God's voice. By going to church and attending various functions there, I was able to meet many devout Christians and heard their testimonies. I was learning that others had heard God's voice or received direction from Him through promptings, signs and "coincidences" (spoiler alert: With God, there are no coincidences—it's Him wonderfully at work). I wasn't the only one in my church having Godly experiences.

I thought there must be a common denominator that would account for these experiences and I didn't think it was in the drinking fountain. I soon realized there were certain principles, we as a church body were being taught and were practicing, that allowed God to be present in the daily lives of those who love him. We weren't observing religion from a distance; we were partaking in a personal relationship with the Lord. Big difference.

If I enjoyed a special connection with God, I knew others would like to experience Him personally as well by learning the same Biblical principles I was being taught. I have a strong suspicion that many people are hungry for a relationship with God, but just don't know how to go about it. Where do you start? In the following pages, I'd like to incorporate some of the principles that have brought me closer to God as I continue with my story.

A relationship with God is no different than a relationship with anybody else; you have to want it and you have to work at it. But it's a relationship where you're allowed to be yourself and you can make mistakes, and God will never leave you. He always gives you another chance. I still stumble and make mistakes all the time. It's called being human and God understands. I don't need to be perfect to be in a relationship with Him. I just have to love Him and let Him love me back.

How do *you* begin to find your own way to a relationship with God? First, you need to understand who God is. God is actually made of three deities: God the Father, God the Son and God the Holy Spirit (The word God is a plural noun, like the word sheep. It refers to three in one). God created the Heavens and the earth and is all knowing, all present, and all powerful. Our God is a holy God of justice and there must be a penalty paid for our sins, which is death. God the Father loves us so much He sent His Son Jesus as a sacrifice for our sins. Jesus paid the penalty. He was crucified, died on the cross in our place, was buried in a tomb, rose again on the third day, and now sits at the right hand of the Father in Heaven. When we believe in Jesus, ask Him to forgive us of our sins, and come into our lives, we have eternal life and Heaven is our home. It's that simple. It's the gift of salvation, we can't earn it, we just have to reach out and accept it.

Do you believe in your heart that Jesus is real, or do you have doubts? I'm here to tell you that He is alive and well—and if you still don't believe in Him, just reread the first six chapters of this book. If my incredible story doesn't convince you, let me tell you something else—I've traveled to the Holy Land and have seen firsthand where Jesus was born, where He taught, where He healed, and where He performed miracles. He really walked this earth two thousand years ago and present-day archeology shows us where. The Bible isn't just an old book full of stories, it's the actual inspired word of God and science is finally catching up with it. Archeologists are continuing to make new discoveries in Israel even today and are using the Bible to validate their findings. So, don't be a doubting Thomas, Jesus is the real deal and you can confidently believe in Him.

I don't know why so many people are afraid to believe in God and let Him in their lives. Jesus tells us, "For God so loved the world that He gave His only begotten Son, that whoever believes in Him should not perish but have everlasting life". In John 3:16 and in John 10:10, Jesus says, "The thief [the devil] does not come except to steal, and to kill, and to destroy. I have come that they may have life, and that they may have it more abundantly."

Now, who wouldn't want everlasting life and life more abundantly while we're spending our time on Earth? Sounds like a winner to me—sign me up!

ON A PRAYER

CHAPTER EIGHT

WHILE I WAS in my mid-fifties, I was growing spiritually, but still dealing with chronic pain issues; this time it was neck and facial pain. I tried physical therapy, but without much improvement. After doing research on the internet, I suspected I might have temporomandibular joint pain (TMJ for short) and sought out my dentist for a second opinion. I knew if my suspicions were right, he would be sending me to a specialist. Dr. Hal had been my dentist for over twenty-five years, and I valued his opinion. I prayed that God would help him diagnosis me correctly and if needed, send me to the right person for healing. After examining me, Doc informed me that my pain was not coming from my jaw, but from my neck and referred me to a headache clinic that treated patients with specialized physical therapy.

When I first arrived at the headache clinic, I was introduced to Angelo, the founder of the clinic, who had a huge list of abbreviations behind his name. He was a physically fit man in his early sixties, with broad shoulders and a positive outlook. Angelo explained to me that he had developed a program for the cervical spine which he taught at medical facilities across the country. It was not like traditional physical therapy; his regimen might take a little longer but was more effective. I wanted to heal without the aids of drugs or surgery, even if it took more time, so I agreed to begin treatment.

Not too long into therapy, I started to notice pain in my right shoulder. It continued to worsen to the point where I couldn't sleep on it or even raise my arm to over my head. I shared my concerns with Angelo, and he made note of it in my records and mentioned the pain could be traveling down from my neck into my shoulder or it could be a mechanical issue within the shoulder joint itself. *Great.*

A couple of weeks went by with no improvement in my shoulder. On the day of my therapy appointment, I was driving to the clinic on the expressway and was thinking about how I've just about had it with all the chronic pain. If you've dealt with pain issues for a lengthy time, you know what I'm talking about. I was angry and I decided to give God a piece of my mind.

"Really, God? Now my shoulder? What, my back and neck weren't enough?! This is starting to get ridiculous! And expensive! I've got chiropractic bills and dentist bills! My insurance has run out and money is flying out the window on this crap." I was more than a little upset. "I don't want to see an orthopedic doctor on this stupid shoulder so he can tell me I need surgery!" I was really getting warmed up.

During my rant, I noticed a big, white SUV passing me in the left lane. This vehicle was speeding so fast, I stopped my tirade to watch it fly by. I noticed its license plate: ASKGOD.

Wow. Attitude adjustment. I guessed I needed to apologize and started over, "Lord, I'm sorry I got carried away. Can you please give me some answers on this shoulder? I don't have the money right now to see an orthopedic and I need your help. I'm scared. Please show me what I need to do to get this fixed, in Jesus name, amen."

I arrived at the headache clinic a little early and took a seat in the waiting room, which was very nice by the way. It was furnished with wingback chairs, a fireplace, fine art, and calming tropical fish scenes on a TV screen.

Angelo came out of his office to greet me and the first words out of his mouth were, "Hi Linda! Hey, do you have some extra time today? The appointment after you just cancelled, and I want to take a look at your shoulder." I had to smile. Our God is a good God. He loves us and hears our prayers, even when we're angry.

Angelo examined my shoulder and determined that my pain was in fact radiating down from my neck, it was not my shoulder. I would not have to go see an orthopedic surgeon. I would not need to dish out more money. I was so relieved! Angelo gave me a few home exercises and within six weeks, my shoulder pain disappeared and hasn't been back since.

I got real with God that day. Was I perfect in my prayer request? No. Could I have acted with more respect? Probably, but I believe God wanted my honest emotion, for it says in Psalms 62:8 "Trust in Him at all times, you people; Pour out your heart before Him; God is a refuge for us." The most memorable prayers for me have been when my emotions were at their rawest. God understands your pain and wants you to come to him with whatever is hurting you. Yes, it might get ugly and yes, there might be tears. You don't have to be perfect in front of God, you need to be respectful, but when things aren't going well you can be authentic with Him. Just be yourself and express what you're really feeling. If you're angry or scared, that's okay, let it out and let God handle it.

Having a prayer life is one of the biblical principles taught in our church. So many people don't know how to pray to God, they think there's some proper way to do it and if they don't say exactly the right thing, God won't listen to them. Not true. Prayer is simply talking to God, just like talking to your best friend. You can tell Him everything and anything, after all He's God and He knows everything about you already. He knows all your needs, all your wants, all your sins, and all your thoughts. He knows where you've been, and He knows where you're going. You can't shock God. You can't surprise God. So why not let Him know exactly what's on your heart?

One afternoon, I was at work, sitting at my desk paying bills. It was during our slow season and money was a little tight. I had pulled all the bills out and was deciding which ones would get paid. Looking at the balance in the checkbook, my mind started to wander. I had been in the photography business all my life and had seen many changes in the business over the years, from hand coloring black and white photos in the 1960's to the present high-tech digital imaging. Our business had always adapted when new technology came along, but the current trends in photography, which made it easily accessible to everyone with camera phones, was really hurting our industry. The drop in revenue was so bad, that many professional photographers were closing their doors. If our sales didn't pick up, we may be one of them.

I was fifty-five years of age and really didn't want to start over and learn a new career. I was sitting in a pity pool and focusing on my lack of income. I started talking to God as I always do. "Father, this doesn't look good. How did so many years of hard work get to this? There's barely enough money here to pay these bills. I know you know where I'm at and what I'm going through, but this is scary. I seriously don't know if we're going to make it."

Surprisingly, I heard a reply, "Do you have enough for today?" It was the Father and it was the first time I heard His magnificent voice. It was different from Jesus' voice. It resonated. I was shocked.

I paused, and then humbly answered, "Yes, Lord."

"Alright then." And that was it.

The Father had just gently chastised me, and I was feeling rather sheepish. I remembered the line in the Lord's Prayer, "Give us this day our daily bread," and in Matthew 6:31-34:

"Therefore do not worry, saying, 'What shall we eat?' or 'What shall we drink?' or 'What shall we wear?' For after all these things the Gentiles seek. For your heavenly Father knows that you need all these things. But seek first the kingdom of God and His righteousness, and all these things shall be added to you. Therefore do not worry about tomorrow, for tomorrow will worry about its own things. Sufficient for the day is its own trouble."

God was right. I had enough for today. There was food on my table and a roof over my head. He had given me my daily bread. These bills would get paid, one at a time, but they would all eventually get paid. I was grateful again for the message, even though I got a little schooling in the process.

This wasn't the first time God reminded me that He had it all under control. Remember when Jesus told me, "Haven't I always taken care of you?" Sometimes, I'm a creature of habit and forget God knows my needs and has them taken care of. If I ever have to change careers, I know God will lead me to where He wants me to be. I can trust in Him for all things, even to remind me when I forget how much He loves me.

If you have worries and concerns, talk to God about it. He cares about every aspect of your life. Nothing is too insignificant for Him. If it matters to you, it matters to God. He wants to be involved with the small things as well as the big things, but He'll only do so when you invite Him into your life. God will never force Himself on you, but He loves you and wants to be included in your everyday comings and goings.

I remember a few winters ago, Bob and I were both experiencing back pain and were going to physical therapy at the same time. We jokingly called it our date night. I was doing one of the many sessions for my herniated disks and Bob recently had the flu where he coughed so hard for so many days, he actually injured his back and was having serious spasms. So here we are, two peas in a pod out of commission, sitting at home on a Sunday afternoon and we get one of our famous Michigan snowstorms. Neither one of us were capable of shoveling the heavy snow. How were we going to get our cars out? We also needed to clear the sidewalk; it was required in our neighborhood. I had no idea what we were going to do, and I was starting to worry about it. I was learning to share my worries with God, so I prayed to Him about it.

A couple of hours later, our doorbell rang. I opened the front door and found two young girls in pink coats standing on my front porch. They looked to be around ten years old. I recognized one of the girls from seeing her around the subdivision.

"Hi, girls!" I said. "What can I do for you?"

One of them spoke up, "We were wondering if we could shovel your driveway for ten dollars."

I smiled. "Of course, you can!" In the twelve years we had lived in that neighborhood, it was the first time anyone had ever asked to shovel our snow. They got to work right away, playing and laughing while they shoveled. I gave them each ten dollars and candy bars as a bonus. God had answered my prayer and sent two little angels in bright, pink coats to help us out. A snow filled driveway might seem like a small thing to pray about, but God didn't think so, He knew it mattered to me.

Now there are ways to make your prayers more effective, like praying to God the Father and ending your prayer in the name of Jesus. The Bible tells us in Colossians 3:17 "And whatever you do in word or deed, do all in the name of the Lord Jesus, giving thanks to God the Father through Him."

Why do we end our prayers with "in Jesus name, Amen"? It was Jesus' finished work on the cross that made us righteous to God the Father and because the only way to the Father is through His Son Jesus, we make our requests in Jesus' name. The name of Jesus also has power. After Jesus ascended back to Heaven, His disciples were able to perform many miracles in His name. We see in Acts 3:6-7 Peter healed a lame man at the gates of the temple, "Then Peter said, 'Silver and gold I do not have, but what I do have I give you: In the name of Jesus Christ of Nazareth, rise up and walk.' And he took him by the right hand and lifted him up, and immediately his feet and ankle bones received strength."

However, God isn't a magic genie in a bottle waiting to grant your every wish. What you ask for needs to go along with His will. Because of that, it may seem that some of your prayers are going unanswered. But don't worry, God hears your request. Trust God to always have your best interest at heart and respond with what's right for you, even if you feel like you're not getting answers.

When I was in my late teens, I fell head over heels for a young man I thought was the one for me. He was everything I ever wanted: tall, dark, and handsome with a charming personality. I begged God to let me marry him; I wanted to spend the rest of my life with this guy. We dated for a while and then he unexpectedly broke off the relationship. I was heartbroken. Why, God, Why? I found out many years later that my first love turned into a man that spent time in jail for serious crimes, had an affair, divorced, and died before he turned forty-five. God clearly had a better plan for my life. I can't imagine what my life would have been like if God let me have my way on that one. Thank God for unanswered prayers.

Learning to pray for His will over your life instead of your own is huge. Proverbs 3:5-6 tells us "Trust in the Lord with all your heart, and lean not on your own understanding; in all your ways acknowledge Him, and He shall direct your paths." God's ways are always better than our ways; after all He can see the whole picture while we can only see what's in front of us.

But it's not always easy to trust God, I get that. That's where faith comes in.   Faith requires us to believe that God is working on our behalf for our greater good, even when we can't see it.

"Blessed is the man who trusts in the Lord, and whose hope is the Lord. For he shall be like a tree planted by the waters, which spreads out its roots by the river, and will not fear when heat comes; but its leaf will be green, and will not be anxious in the year of draught, nor will cease from yielding fruit," Jeremiah 17:7-8.

Because all things are possible with God, we can trust Him to find a way when we can't. Jesus tells us in Luke 18:27 "The things which are impossible with men are possible with God." Trusting in God gives you a peace only He can give you. I've learned that life goes a lot better when we let God do the driving.

Our faith is so important to God, He will even reward us when we believe in Him, as He tells us in Hebrews 11:6 " But without faith it is impossible to please Him, for he who comes to God must believe that He is, and that He is a rewarder of those who diligently seek Him." Completely trusting God takes time, just like in any relationship. But unlike any relationship you've ever had, He won't ever let you down.

1 Thessalonians 5:16-18 tells us to "Rejoice always, *pray without ceasing*, in everything give thanks; for this is the will of God in Christ Jesus for you." I talk to God throughout the day—in the shower, in the car, cooking dinner. I even talk to

God when I'm in line at the grocery store. Most of the time, I only have a simple request, a quick comment to share, or I'll just take a second to tell Jesus I love Him. If I see someone who needs God's help, I'll pause and pray right where I'm at and then go on about my day. Before I go to bed, I thank the Lord for the blessings of the day and pray for the people on my prayer list. I enjoy sharing my day with God. It helps me to know He's always with me.

So, by praying to God, you can begin to build a closer relationship with Him by asking for His help, sharing your life, and thanking Him for your blessings. But I don't believe God wants it to be a one-sided conversation where you do all the talking and He can't get a word in edge wise. Remember, a relationship takes two. I think He wants to be heard as well, and when we take a little time to slow down and listen, it's very possible to hear God's voice.

If you think hearing God's voice is scary or out of your realm, think about what Jesus tells us in John 14:21 "He who has My commandments and keeps them, it is he who loves Me. And he who loves Me will be loved by My Father, and I will love him and manifest Myself to him," and as we saw earlier in John 10:27 "My sheep hear My voice…"

So, why is it so crazy to think you can literally hear from Jesus? He just told you He'll manifest himself to those who love Him. He didn't say you have to be a guru of spirituality to hear Him, you just have to love Him. But how do you go about hearing God's voice? I'm glad you asked.

I use prayer and meditation combined together and it's a wonderful way to be in the presence of the Lord. Medical research confirms that meditation is beneficial to your health and we all know that prayer is beneficial to your soul, so the prayer meditation combo is a win-win. It's me time with a plus—I have an opportunity to hear from God. I usually only pray meditate when I'm having an issue with a situation and need to hear Jesus' voice on the matter. I find when I am emotionally driven with a question, have pondered on it for a while, and then sincerely seek Him for guidance, He responds in some way to my plea.

The prayer meditation is a little more intense than your everyday prayers and conversations with God. It's your heart talking to His and it's beautiful. To get started, you need to find a quiet place where you won't be interrupted, like a bedroom or a study. Settle in a comfortable sitting position, close your eyes and concentrate on your breathing. Let your body relax and try to calm the thoughts running through your mind. That's a tough one. Our minds are constantly going, so if you have trouble with the influx of thoughts, focus on the inhaling and exhaling of your breath.

Then, begin a prayer. I like to start my prayer with a list of things I'm grateful for. It's important at this time that you ask God to protect you from any other voices that may try to interfere such as the devil or even your own thoughts. You want to hear from God and God alone. I recommend you even ask for protection out loud to make sure any outside spiritual influences get the message to stay away.

Then, ask your question. What do you ask Him? Anything that's on your mind. I've asked Him why particular things have happened in my past, what He wants me to do in a current situation, or how I can strengthen my relationship with Him. I've asked Him for guidance, wisdom, healing, and assurance. You can bring your genuine concerns to God and seek His assistance with anything you're going through.

Once you've asked your specific question, let God know you would appreciate a response from Him and finish your prayer in Jesus name, Amen. Your prayer might go something like this:

"Dear Jesus,

Thank you for your sacrifice on the cross. Thank you for forgiving my sins and making Heaven my home. Please protect me from any outside influences and interruptions today so I may clearly hear any message You may have for me. Dear Lord, I have a question that I need Your help with. Can you please tell me (fill in your question)? I would greatly appreciate your wisdom and guidance on this issue. Thank you. In Your name I pray. Amen."

Then wait and continue breathing with your eyes closed. Let go of any expectations you might have. You may not hear God's voice right away, but you may have other signs of communication. You might get a feeling, or you might see a picture, just be open to what comes. If you don't get any results the first time, don't be disappointed, just try again another time. The prayer meditation is like anything else, the more you practice, the better you get.

How do you know if what you're experiencing is from God and not another source? God will never contradict Himself. Use the Bible as your reference book and compare the messages you're receiving with what God's Word says. God will never tell you to divorce your spouse or steal to pay the rent. His spoken word will always be consistent with Scripture. Remember Jesus' first words to me, "I never left you"? It says in Hebrews 13:5 "…For He Himself has said, 'I will never leave you nor forsake you'." Take the time to verify the messages you are receiving. It's worth the effort to make sure you're actually hearing God's voice and not your own wishful thinking.

When I began to write this book, I was having doubts if I could accomplish such a task. I knew God wanted me to share my testimony, but I wasn't a professional writer, I was just a person with a story. I took my concerns to God in a prayer meditation. After saying a prayer of gratitude and protection from outside influences, I talked to Jesus about my fears:

"Lord, am I even supposed to write this book? I'm not really qualified. I'm not a professional and this is harder than I thought. I don't think I can write enough pages to fill a book." I was sincerely honest with Him and patiently waited for any type of response.

I heard His caring voice, "You have been anointed and given the tools you need."

I searched the Bible and found in 1 John 2:27 "But the anointing which you have received from Him abides in you, and you do not need that anyone teach you; but as the same anointing teaches you concerning all things, and is true, and is not a lie, and just as it has taught you, you will abide in Him."

I no longer had to doubt myself; God just validated that, through Him, I had what it takes to get this book written. And once again, He was right. With a computer, spell check, thesaurus, the Bible, and the Holy Spirit, I had all the tools I needed. Jesus had graciously told me to quit doubting myself and trust Him to equip me for the job.

I'm grateful for my prayers and meditations with the Lord. They give me peace, hope, guidance, strength and joy that only a relationship with God can give you. By taking time every day to share my life with God, I don't worry over the things as I used to, and I enjoy the journey so much more. It's one of the best things you can do for yourself and those you love—I highly recommend it.

IN A WORD

CHAPTER NINE

I WOULD LIKE TO share with you an illustration God gave me in a prayer meditation. Imagine that it's your birthday. You're surrounded by friends and family and you are about to eat cake and open presents. It's a delightful day. There's a little girl in your life that has made a treasured gift for you. She's so excited to see you open it, she can't wait. She made this gift with her own hands and put her heart and soul in it. She gives you her gift with a big smile of anticipation; she really hopes you love it.

You carefully open the gift. It's a painting. She enthusiastically explains it's a picture she drew of you and her, your house, and the sun. You love the fact that she painted it for you. You would never throw the painting away; it would break her heart. You take the painting and proudly display it on your refrigerator so you can be reminded everyday of your relationship with her and how much she loves you.

God has a similar gift for you, but it's a picture of you and *Him*, *His* house, and *His* Son. It's called the Bible and He made it with His heart and soul because He loves you. Are you going to throw it away or enjoy it every day and be reminded of your relationship with God and how much He loves you?

But why is reading the Bible so important in your relationship with God? You pray already, isn't that enough? Praying to the Lord is essential in developing your relationship

with Him, that's true, but what do you really know about
God? Who is this entity you pray to; do you really know
Him? Wouldn't you like to? By reading God's Word, you are
implementing another biblical principle in your relationship
with Him. Jesus Himself took time to learn the Scriptures
because He knew the importance of it, "But He answered and
said, 'It is written, '*Man shall not live by bread alone, but by
every word that proceeds from the mouth of God*" Matthew 4:4.
The Bible will tell you everything you want to know about the
God who loves you, along with all His desires and blessings for
your life.

I can hear you groaning already. "*Read* the Bible? It's
so outdated and hard to read. Who talks like that anymore?
I can't understand it. I read those stories when I was a kid, I
don't need to read them again."

Okay, I hear you. But just in case you're wondering, the
Bible is full of God's promises and blessings for your life.
Here's just a few of the good things God has in store for you:

Eternal life	John 3:16
Wisdom	James 1:5
Peace	John 14:27
Strength	Philippians 4:13
Protection	Psalm 91
Blessings	Matthew 7:11
Provision	Philippians 4:19
Rewards	Hebrews 11:6
Rest	Matthew 11:28
Guidance	Proverbs 3:6
Joy	John 15:11
Healing	1 Peter 2:24

Plus, the Bible is a fascinating book filled with action,

romance, scandal, mystery, and so much more—and the best part is, it's all true! Who needs fiction when you have the real stories of the Bible? And the self-help sections are amazing! You don't have to go through *anything* alone—God is always with you, and He's got an answer for every situation. After all, He created us. How thoughtful of Him to give us an owner's manual for all of life's emergencies.

"But I can't make heads or tails out of that old language with all those thou's and hath's," you say. I have a hard time with those words myself. Lucky for us, there are over forty versions of the Bible in English alone. Now, a version of the Bible doesn't mean a different Bible, there's only one Bible, it refers to the translation style. The original Scriptures of the Old Testament were written in ancient Hebrew and the New Testament was originally written in Greek. Scholars have been able to translate these original writings into present day language and, depending on the version, they ring pretty true to the original Scriptures. The New King James Version (NKJV) and the New American Standard Version (NASV) are believed to be very accurate translations of the original writings. I used the New King James Version for the quotes in this book.

So, get busy and go get yourself a Bible! If you have a Christian bookstore near you, go in and look at the different Bibles until you find one that feels "just right" or check out online stores to find your perfect match from the comfort of your own living room. You can also download a Bible to your smartphone, (yes, there *is* an app for that!) or download a version on your tablet or computer. Many of the downloads are free and yours for the taking!

I firmly believe God is present and reaches out to us when we open His book and read His word. The Bible may have sixty-six books written by forty different authors, but it is all inspired by God Himself.

"All Scripture is given by inspiration of God, and is profitable for doctrine, for reproof, for correction, for instruction in righteousness, that the man of God may be complete, thoroughly equipped for every good work" 2 Timothy 3:16-17. There have been many times, when I have been reading a verse in the Bible and felt like God was talking directly to me and helping me address an issue at hand.

There have also been times when I have prayed over an issue, randomly opened the Bible and the answer I needed was on the first page I looked at. Now I'm not suggesting that the Bible is some magical book that you can open and instantly get the perfect answer to your problem. Be careful with that one, there are a lot of verses that can be taken out of context and get you into trouble. Take time to read the entire passage before determining if God is speaking to your heart.

If you are sincere about finding God's answer for your problem, research what His Word has to say about it. To help you, many Bibles have sections in the front that will refer you to verses for the situation you're dealing with. Or you can search Christian websites on the internet by asking your search engine," What does the Bible says about _____ (fill in the blank)?"

But you say," The Bible is so difficult for me. I don't understand the culture from two thousand years ago and the parables Jesus taught make no sense to me." No problem! There are excellent books called Bible Commentaries that give you a run-down of the entire Bible and will help you understand any questions that may arise. There are also Study Bibles that present the scripture and corresponding comments on each page, so you can learn as you go. See, God knows your concerns and is already a step ahead of you!

So, now that you've decided to crack that big book open, where do you start? Do you have to start at the beginning and read it from front to back? Nope, you can start wherever you want. The Bible wasn't written like a novel where you need to read it in chronological order. The Old Testament (the Old Covenant) are the books before Jesus walked the earth and contains books of history, books of wisdom, books of poetry and books of prophesy. The New Testament (the New Covenant) contains the Gospels, the Epistles or letters, and the book of Revelation (on what is yet to come).

I suggest you start in the New Testament with one of the Gospels of Matthew, Mark, Luke or John. Each one of these books gives a detailed account of Jesus' life and direct quotes from Jesus are included. I often open the Bible to one of the gospels and read Jesus' spoken word, just to be in His presence and hear His voice. He has so many messages to guide us and encourage us; I normally don't let a day go by without reading something Jesus taught.

Another good place to start is in the Old Testament at the very beginning in the book of Genesis. It was written by Moses and contains many famous Biblical celebrities including Adam and Eve, Noah, Abraham, Isaac, Jacob, and Joseph. I usually keep two bookmarks in my Bible, one in the Old Testament and one in the New Testament because I like to read a little from both sections daily.

Wherever you start, when you read the Bible, slow down and take your time. Don't read the book like a newspaper where you skim the headlines and just look for a few details. Savor what you're reading. Meditate on it. Imagine what was really happening in the verses you're studying. What was going through these people's minds? How were their lives affected? How does what you're reading apply to *your* life? If you read just one verse and meditate on it, you'll benefit more

than if you rush through a whole page. Enjoy your Bible time,
it's not a race, you're allowed to stop and smell the roses.

The Bible is such a magnificent book; it can be as simple or
as complex as you want. You can take the beautiful messages at
face value or dig deeper for more in depth study. The writings
are full of symbolism, parables and hidden messages. Even the
use of names and numbers can have a significant meaning.
One of my favorite stories takes place after Jesus' resurrection
on the cross. The disciples decide to go fishing at night but
catch nothing. On their way back to shore in the morning,
they spot someone on the shore. This man asks them if they
have any food and when they reply no, the stranger tells them
to cast their nets over to the right side of the boat. They do so
and catch an astounding one hundred and fifty-three fish. The
disciples realize it is the resurrected Jesus, who then asks them
for some of the fish and proceeds to cook breakfast for them.
The entire story is in the book of John. I always wondered, why
one-hundred-and-fifty-three fish? Someone had to count all
those fish, why would God choose to share that detail?

I don't know, but here's a fun fact—someone did the math
and found that one-hundred-and-fifty-three people were
individually recognized as being blessed by Jesus in the four
gospels: three people in the book of Mark, forty-seven people
in Matthew, ninety-four people in Luke and nine people in
John. It's recognized that the number one-hundred-and-fifty-
three symbolizes God's overflowing blessings.

The number one-hundred-and-fifty-three has a special
meaning for me as well. It started with a visit to the dentist.
When Bob and I decided to visit Israel with our church group,
I wanted to get my teeth checked before we traveled. I was not
a faithful, see-my-dentist-every-six-months, kind of person. I
don't know about you, but I'm not a big fan of dentists with
their drills, their shots, and all their metal instruments. But

my dentist, Dr. Hal, makes a visit with him as painless as he possibly can. He's a very kind and gracious man who never scolds me for neglecting my teeth. It had been a while since I had been to his office and I thought if I was smart, I'd make sure my teeth were in good condition before I flew half way around the world; I didn't need any surprises in the Middle East.

After x-rays were taken and my mouth examined, it was determined I was in tremendous need of a cleaning, plus two fillings and possibly two crowns. *Cha-Ching.* My dental work was broken up into series of appointments and would take over a month to complete. The cleaning alone took four appointments and cost close to one thousand dollars (I've since learned my lesson, and now go twice a year).

Money was starting to pour out and, with the expenses of our upcoming trip, I was starting to get nervous about the bills once again (I'm a slow learner). I had one final dentist appointment to get through. Doc said he wasn't sure if the last visit would entail a filling or a crown, and he wouldn't know until he started drilling on my tooth. If you've ever had dental work done, you know there's a big difference in the price of a filling and a crown. Like a thousand dollars difference.

On the day of my last appointment, I arrived at Dr. Hal's office and one of his cheerful dental assistants showed me to the dental chair, laid out the instruments needed for my procedure, then left me to myself to wait for Doc. I took the opportunity to pray. "Dear Lord, please let this be a filling. You know how much money I've had to spend on my teeth. I know all things are possible with you and if you could swing this, I would be truly grateful, in Jesus name, Amen."

Dr. Hal entered the room with his usual smile and a handshake.

After a brief conversation, he asked, "Ready to get started?"

No, I thought, *I'd rather sit here and chitchat.*

Once he had me numbed up, he got the drill out and said, "Well, let's see what we've got." Please, Lord, please let it be a filling. "Good news, Linda!" he exclaimed. "Looks like we can get away with just a filling today. It's not as bad as I thought." I was so relieved; I thanked God right in the dental chair!

Once Dr. Hal was finished, we said our goodbyes and I proceeded to the front counter to pay my bill. When the receptionist handed me the bill, I had to laugh. The amount was one-hundred-and-fifty-three dollars. God had just answered my prayer and gave me a smile to let me know the blessing was from Him.

I then started to see one-hundred-and-fifty-three pop up in other places. About a week later, I received my medical insurance explanation in the mail and noticed Angelo's office was charging my insurance one-hundred-and-fifty-three dollars per therapy visit. Angelo personally knew Dr. Hal; they were friends outside of their medical realm. So, on my next visit with Angelo, I shared the Bible story of Jesus and the one-hundred-and-fifty-three fish and how that number was showing up on his bill as well as Doc's. We both felt it wasn't a coincidence.

"God's up to something with my healing and the two of you," I told him. "I think God wants us to know He's got a hand in this." As we were wrapping up my visit, I lightheartedly made the comment to Angelo on my way out the door, "Remember, God's still in this." Driving home that day from the clinic, I found myself behind a car with the license plate GODINUS! Another smile from God.

Not long after, I had to take my dog to the veterinarian. He was getting up there in years and was receiving geriatric care with a special diet and blood pressure medication. While I was waiting in the vet's lobby, I started to think about a

Christian organization I was interested in joining that takes therapy dogs into all sorts of places like nursing homes and hospitals to share God's love. My dog was too old to become a therapy dog, but I was contemplating getting a second dog I could train. I noticed on the vet's bulletin board a flyer for a dog trainer in my area that was able to train and qualify dogs for therapy work. I was so excited to find a training source; I immediately wrote all the information down. After our appointment, I'm at the front desk paying my bill and you guessed it—it's one-hundred-and-fifty-three dollars. I guess God likes the idea of using dogs in His ministry because He just smiled on me once again. If I hadn't spent time reading the Bible and meditating on God's word, I would have missed God's interaction with me on those three occasions.

Reading the Bible is a wonderful way to connect with the Lord and strengthen your relationship with Him. God has so many blessings for your life and wants to share them all with you. He wants you to know that you can trust Him, and He loves you more than you've ever been loved before. He wants to guide you to a better, more abundant happy life. You're special to God and He's given you a beautiful gift in His written word because He wants you to be close to Him. Get in the habit of finding time to read the Scriptures, even if it's only one verse a day, it will make a huge difference in your life. It did mine.

LET YOUR LIGHT SHINE

CHAPTER TEN

WHEN JESUS TOLD me that it was time to do His work, I didn't know what He meant. I couldn't figure it out. He told me I was to teach and inspire and we left it at that. I knew God had a purpose for my life and when the timing was right, He would reveal His plan to me. And one day He did. It all started with a little drawing of a hummingbird.

It was Christmas time, and I was still seeking treatment for my neck pain with Angelo. I like to give my therapists presents, especially at Christmas, as I am grateful for all their help with my healing. I decided to give Angelo a restaurant gift card but didn't feel it was personal enough. At the time, I was doing some miniature pen and ink sketches of various animals. One of the little drawings was of a hummingbird and something said, Give that to Angelo.

I thought, *No, that's crazy. What is a big guy like Angelo going to do with a little picture of a hummingbird?* But the thought persisted. So, I put the drawing in a magnet frame and added it to the gift card.

When I gave Angelo the hummingbird drawing, he made over it like one of his own kid's had drawn it, which I appreciated. As an artist, there's always insecurity when you give a piece of your art and it's something I rarely do, because I don't want to make someone feel they have to be polite and say "I love it!" when they might not. But Angelo said he liked it and thanked me for the sketch more than once. The following week, he told me he actually put it on his refrigerator at home; I guess he really did like it!

Three months go by, and I had an appointment with Angelo on March 16th, four days before Bob and I were to leave for the Holy Land. As Christians, we celebrate 3:16 Day because it reminds us of John 3:16 "For God so loved the world that He gave His only begotten Son, that whoever believes in Him should not perish but have everlasting life." It's the most recognized verse in the Bible and is used to help bring many people to Christ.

The therapy session was going along as usual, when Angelo pulled out his cell phone and said, "Can I show you something? In my thirty-five years in practice, I've never done this, but I thought as an artist, you might appreciate it." He definitely had my attention. "I'm also an artist. I was an art major in college before I decided to get into medicine," he added as he proceeded to show me some of his magnificent pastel paintings on his phone. I was stunned! They were professional quality. "Please don't tell anyone here at the clinic," he said. "I don't share my personal life with the people I work with and they don't know about my art. Something just said for me to share this with you." (There's that *something* again!)

I was blown away. How could he have that much talent and hide it like a light under a basket! I thought of the verse:

"Nor do they light a lamp and put it under a basket, but on a lampstand, and it gives light to all who are in the house. So let your light shine before men, that they may see your good works and glorify your Father in heaven" Matthew 5:15-16. As a fellow artist, you would give anything to have a gift like that; some artists go their whole lives and never accomplish what he just showed me, and he wasn't doing anything with it! Before

I left his office that day, I gave Angelo a piece of my mind, in a nice but enthusiastic way, of course, on how he should be using his talents.

The conversation with Angelo really affected me, so much so, when I went to bed that night, it was still on my mind.

I took it to God in prayer, "Father, I don't know why Angelo and his art bothers me so badly. It's not my business if he uses his talents or not. I guess I just don't understand how You could give him such a gift and he hid it under a basket and doesn't even share it with his coworkers. Why is this affecting me so much?"

Surprisingly, I heard God's voice, "Listen to your own words. What gift have I given *you* that *you* have hidden under a basket and have not shared with *your* coworkers?" Oh—oh. I knew God wasn't talking about my art, because I share my art with my coworkers. He was talking about His Son Jesus. It was 3:16 Day and God just asked me to share with others the personal experiences I had with His Son.

I wasn't ready for that. I had been hiding my experiences for a long time and the thought of sharing my story scared me to death. I felt like Moses at the burning bush when God asked him to lead His people out of Egypt. I was reluctant to be given the mission, had a slew of reasons why I wasn't the right person for the job, but in the end knew when God says go, you go.

"Okay Lord, but you're going to have to lead me," is all I could respond with.

I went into work the next day, met with my business partner, and nervously told him my entire Jesus story. It felt good to finally get my secret out in the open.

He took it better than I expected and replied with, "Well, that explains a lot of things." At the end of the day, he wished me well on my trip to the Holy Land and two days later, Bob and I were touring in Israel with our church group.

The sights we saw in the Holy Land were amazing. We took a boat ride on the Sea of Galilee, walked the streets of Old Jerusalem, and were even baptized in the Jordan River. As we took communion at the Garden Tomb (a believed site of Jesus' burial), I thought about God's words and knew that just sharing Jesus with my business partner wasn't enough. God wanted more out of me and He was working on my heart about it.

When we returned home from our adventures in Israel, Pastor started a series of sermons on the Great Commission taught by Jesus, "And He said to them, 'Go into all the world and preach the gospel to every creature'," Mark 16:15. Pastor encouraged us to witness and share our testimonies in the hopes of bringing others to Christ. I had not yet shared my story with Pastor, and I was beginning to wonder why he presently chose this particular message to teach. Coincidence? I think we know better. God was talking directly to me through Pastor's preaching and trust, me I was squirming in my pew.

I knew I needed to submit to God and share my testimony; this was His plan for me. But how was I going to tell my story? Telling strangers or acquaintances I've seen Jesus would put me in the "crazy lady" category and might do more harm than good. But I did think people might understand my story in a book (you know me and books). So, I invited Pastor and his wife over for dinner to get their opinion and, well, you know the rest.

Did I eagerly accept the Lord's plan for me? No. God had to work on my heart until my desire was so strong, I knew I had no other choice but to submit to His calling. But, like Moses, God has been with me every step of the way and has given me the tools I need to accomplish the mission. I had mistakenly hidden my light under a basket for so many years. Now, I look forward to telling my story in the hopes that souls will get saved and many will come to love the Lord.

When I started to write my first pages, I did a prayer meditation and asked Jesus what He wanted me to say with this book.

He replied, "Show them how much you love Me." I sincerely hope I've done that. If you decide to Love Jesus and let Him in your heart, here's a prayer of salvation you can pray to accept Jesus as your Personal Savior right now, right where you are. Just repeat the following prayer:

Dear Father God,

I understand that I am a sinner and I ask forgiveness of my sins. I believe that Jesus Christ is Your Son and He died on the cross in my place, was buried in the tomb, rose again on the third day, and now sits at your right hand. I accept Jesus as my Lord and Savior and I repent of my sins. I ask that you come into my life and make Heaven my home. In Jesus name, I pray. Amen.

If you prayed that simple prayer, congratulations! You are now a child of God! It's that simple. To further your relationship with God, spend time in prayer, read the Bible, and find your way to a Bible based church.

Have you thought about attending church? I know what you're thinking, for years I balked at the idea of it. Every time I called my Aunt Marsha, she would ask if I had found a church yet. She never gave up. I didn't understand why she thought it was so important for me, until I started going.

Church has so many benefits, I don't know where to begin. First, you have the opportunity to worship God in His house. You can say a prayer on Holy ground and know you are in God's presence. I can't explain it, but there is a blessing that you can only receive by being in the house of the Lord. There have been so many times, I have walked into church with chronic pain and during the service, my pain was gone. Coincidence? I don't think so. I'm not suggesting that going to church will cure your aches and illnesses, but there's something transforming about worshipping God in church with other believers. Being able to praise God in His house is a special privilege and I always look forward to it.

Second, you hear biblically based messages that will improve your life and teach you the Scriptures. It's like having your own personal life coach. By listening to the teachings, you are given the spiritual tools you need to navigate through this crazy world and be successful by God's methods, which have been tried and true for thousands of years. Church sermons give you motivation and encouragement to help you get out there and tackle the world head on.

Third, you have support from the pastor and other Christians. If you need counseling, most pastors have had Biblical training in helping people with their problems. And if you need a friend, the church is full of them! Many of my church friends started out as someone who sat next to me during a Sunday morning service. What started out as a "Hi. How you doing?" has, over time, turned into treasured friendships.

And fourth, it gives you an opportunity to serve God and give back. There are lots of ways to serve the Lord in a church, from singing in the choir, to helping with special projects, to lending a hand in the kitchen or classrooms. It feels good to be able to give back and be a blessing to others and God appreciates it too!

I enjoy going to church so much that I tell people I don't *have* to go to church—I *get* to go to church. If you are currently in a church and don't feel that way about it, I suggest you start shopping around. There are a lot of thriving churches out there where the Bible is taught, and the church community will welcome you and make you part of the family. Church should be an enjoyable place where you feel the love of God, can receive the help you need, and get inspired to be a better version of yourself.

If you're not able to regularly attend church, you can still strengthen your relationship with God. How about watching sermons on TV? There are many good preachers on the Christian channels that teach the Bible and have wonderful messages. With the variety of different preaching styles available, you can find a pastor you feel comfortable with, whether it's laid back or raise the roof, Hallelujah!

Another beneficial tool to bring you closer to God is called a daily devotional. Devotionals are usually short, inspirational messages with a corresponding Bible verse. They only take a minute to read and are positive and uplifting. Many nationally recognized pastors have devotionals on their website, and you can sign up to have them sent to your email or Facebook account for free. A quick search on the internet and you can find an assortment of devotionals to choose from.

Another inspirational tool is Christian music. I'm not talking about the old- fashioned church Hymns, (unless you like those), I'm talking about the contemporary Christian music you can find on the radio. The musicians and the messages are outstanding, and the style is so mainstream, I can have it playing on my computer at work and my employees don't even notice that it's not Pop radio. I don't know how many times I've been in the car with the radio on and the perfect song came on with the exact message I needed to hear. Coincidence? By now I think you know the answer. God uses music in His ministry too. So, don't be afraid to try a new radio station with positive, uplifting messages designed to help you with your Christian walk. It's a fun way to worship the Lord and keep Him front and center throughout your day.

God uses a variety of tools to help you maintain a relationship with Him including prayer, the Bible, church, TV sermons, devotionals, music and other Christians—all because He loves you. He loves you so much that He sent Jesus to die on the cross so that your sins can be forgiven, and you can make Heaven your home. That's a big love. You are very important to God and He doesn't want you to slip through the cracks. God wants to shine His light on you and bless you beyond your wildest dreams. He wants to see your light shine as well. He wants you to be the best you can be, and He has a plan and a purpose for your life.

If you take one message from my story, let it be this: God loves you, He'll never give up on you, and He wants to be with you always! Enjoy your connection with the Lord—it's for eternity!

IN CONCLUSION

WHEN I STARTED this journey so long ago, I didn't have all the answers. I still don't. But I do know this—Jesus is real. I've seen Him and heard Him and felt His amazing love and grace. I also know that Hell exists because I've experienced the demons who disguised themselves as spirit guides trying to lure me away from the truth. Jesus is the Truth and the Way. Not cosmic entities. Not one with the Universe. Not fate. Jesus.

I hope after reading my story that you are inspired to have a closer relationship with the Lord. Please don't walk away and turn your back on the most important decision of your life, because you are going to spend eternity somewhere and it's your choice—Heaven or Hell.

Jesus said in John 14:1-6: "Let not your heart be troubled; you believe in God, believe also in Me. In My Father's house are many mansions, if it were not so, I would have told you. I go to prepare a place for you. And if I go and prepare a place for you, I will come again and receive you to Myself; that where I am, there you may be also. And where I go you know, and the way you know."

Thomas said to Him, "Lord, we do not know where You are going, and how can we know the way?"

Jesus said to him, "I am the way, the truth, and the life. No one comes to the Father except through Me."

Jesus loves us more than we'll ever know. He died on the cross for all our sins so that we may have a place in Heaven. He wants to be a part of our lives. He wants to provide, protect, teach, lead, inspire, heal, and comfort us. It's a free gift that, as sinners, we don't deserve but is ours for the asking.

I'm so glad I let Jesus into my life. I draw nearer to Him through prayer, reading His Word and worshipping in His house. God draws nearer to me because I choose to spend quality time with Him, and He loves me. He loves you too. Always know that. It's a big love and God knows you're worth it. If you haven't already, start a relationship with Him. It will be the best decision you'll ever make!

UPDATE

L INDA CONTINUES TO paint for the Lord and volunteer at her church. She is now writing Christian books for children and teaching Sunday School on a regular basis. She comments that, "Teaching kids about God and His magnificent love for us is the best thing I've ever done with my life. I thank Jesus for giving me the opportunity to share His message with His children. It's both humbling and amazing. What an awesome God we serve!"

NOTES

CHAPTER 2

Page 13. "dreams where an angel or God spoke…" Matthew 2:13, Numbers 12:6

Page 13. "prophetic dreams that needed to be interpreted…" Genesis 41:15-16

CHAPTER 3

Page 27. "Jesus loves us unconditionally…" Romans 8:37-39

Page 28. "God's dislike of mediums…" Deuteronomy 18:10-12

Page 34. "the birds Jesus spoke of…" Matthew 6:26

Page 34. "as Christians, we are to recognize the needs of others…" James 1:27, Philippians 2:3-4

Page 40. "devil was once an angel named Lucifer…" Isaiah 14:12-14, Revelation 12:7-9

CHAPTER 5

Page 45. "with God's grace, we are automatically saved when we accept Jesus…" John 3:16

CHAPTER 6

Page 54. "Jesus is with us all the time." Matthew 28:20

Page 55. " It's very important to Him…" Mark 12:30

Page 56. "That's what He wants from all of us…" Mark 12:30

Page 60. "He always give you another chance. Lamentations 3:21-23, 1 John 1:9

CHAPTER 7

Page 60. "God is made of three deities…" Matthew 28:19

Page 60. "Our God is a holy God of justice…" Ecclesiastes 12:14

Page 60. "God created the Heavens and the earth…" Genesis 1:1

Page 60. "is all knowing and all present…" Proverbs 15:3

Page 60. "a penalty paid for our sins, which is death." Romans 6:23

Page 60. "Jesus paid the penalty." Romans 5:6-10

Page 60. "When we believe in Jesus…" Mark 1:15

Page 61. "gift of salvation…" Ephesians 2:8

Page 61. "actual inspired word of God…" 2 Timothy 3:16

Page 61. "archeologists…using the Bible to validate their

findings." Eric Metaxas, "Archeologists used the Bible to search for Naboth's vineyard and now they've found it" Nov 2017, Christian Today, www.christiantoday.com/article/archeoliogists-used-the-bible-search-for-naboth (January 2018)

CHAPTER 8

Page 67. "I remembered the line in the Lord's Prayer..." Matthew 6:9-13

Page 71. "Medical research confirms that meditation is beneficial..." Susan Kuchinskas, Meditation Heals Body and Mind, 2009, WebMD, www.webmd.com/balance/features/meditation-heals-body-and-minds#1, (January 2018)

Page 73. "God will never contradict Himself." Titus 1:2

CHAPTER 9

Page 77. "He's got an answer for every situation." 2 Timothy 3:16-17

Page 77. "40 versions of the Bible in English alone." Why are there different versions of the Bible?, 2017, The Interactive Bible, www.bible.ca/b-many-versions.htm (February 2018)

Page 77. "The original scriptures of the Old Testament were written in..." Ibid.

Page 77. "The New King James version and the New American Standard..." Ibid.

Page 80. "153 people were individually recognized as being blessed..." The Number 153, The Meaning of Numbers in the Bible, The Bible Study Site, www.biblestudy.org, (February 2018)

CHAPTER 10

Page 86. "It's the most recognized verse in the Bible..." John 3:16 Bible Rank 1, 2014, topverses.com, https://topverses.com/bible/john/3/16, (February 2018)

Page 87. "Moses at the burning bush..." Exodus 3 -4:12

Page 92. "He wants to bless you..." 2 Corinthians 9:8

Page 92. "He has a plan and purpose for your life..." Jeremiah 29:11

Linda being photographed by her father at their home studio in the 1960's.

Linda's mother giving a photo hand coloring demonstration
in the 1960's, using a portrait of Linda.

Linda at age 17 with one of their Arabian mares and foal.

Linda's High School Senior Portrait with one of her German
Shepherds, taken by her father in 1979.

Linda and Bob's wedding in 1992.

Linda in the casino on her honeymoon.

Linda at her studio holding a photo of herself at age three
sitting at her mother's desk.

Linda with Angelo holding the hummingbird sketch
she gave him for Christmas.

Linda and Bob on the Sea of Galilee, Israel in 2017.

Linda, Bob, and Pastor in Israel, 2017.

CPSIA information can be obtained
at www.ICGtesting.com
Printed in the USA
LVHW081944081120
671086LV00010B/899

9 781642 379433